PRAISE FOR GROUND

"Ground is beautifully written and deeply resonant, the kind of gentle wisdom that can guide you through every stage of life. If you're seeking peace or a compass for your journey, this is the book you need." — **Kendall Taylor, Firefighter & Non-Profit Leader**

"Vignettes of grit, determination, survival, confrontation, and change permeate insights on how to effect meaningful change and new directions in life. More so than most spiritual, philosophical, or firefighting accounts, *Ground* documents various paths to achievement and a better life. It should be on the reading lists of anyone interested in actively effecting positive change in their lives." – **D. Donovan, Senior Reviewer, Midwest Book Review**

"For young people navigating the sound and fury of modern life, Ground is a pivotal guidebook. Using a compass forged from lived experience, Kelly McCoy leads us through mazes of uncertainty and into the light of grace and resilience." — **Zeke Holm, English & Philosophy Graduate, Camp Youth Leader, Catalina Island, CA**

"Ground: A Firefighter's Philosophy for Living is a thoughtful, deeply personal guide to navigating life with stability, presence, and purpose. With anecdotes from high-stakes rescues and reflections on building emotional and mental resilience, the book becomes more than a memoir and transforms into a manual for grounded living... true strength comes not from avoiding life's flames, but from standing firm in the midst of them." — **K.C. Finn, Readers' Favorite 5-Star Review**

"Ground is not a quick read; it is meant to be reflected upon and revisited. It will appeal to first responders, veterans, and anyone drawn to honest reflections on resilience, purpose, and healing. It's ideal for those navigating grief, stress, or spiritual searching, and especially meaningful to parents, educators, and men exploring identity and strength." — **Carol Thompson, Readers' Favorite 5-Star Review**

"Ground: A Firefighter's Philosophy for Living is a clear and, forgive the pun, grounded work that offers plenty of wisdom rooted in author Kelly McCoy's life experiences... this book feels like an honest conversation that puts its highest value on authenticity. Recommended." — **Asher Syed, Readers' Favorite 5-Star Review**

"Ground holds a treasure trove of wisdom! Writing for an audience of young adults, McCoy includes tips for successful living that, at 78, I intend to use." — **Marilyn Pilkey, Oread Friends, Lawrence, Kansas**

GROUND

A FIREFIGHTER'S PHILOSOPHY FOR LIVING

KELLY MCCOY

DISCLAIMER

I am not a licensed therapist, physician, financial advisor, or spiritual teacher. I'm a retired firefighter, a father, and a student of life. This book reflects my personal experiences, stories, and insights—offered not as professional advice, but as reflections from a life lived fully, honestly, and sometimes painfully.

The practices and ideas in these pages—on breath work, resilience, safety, spirituality, relationships, and economics—are shared in good faith. They reflect my understanding at the time of writing and may not apply to everyone's unique circumstances. They are not intended as substitutes for therapy, medical care, or financial counsel. Please consult qualified professionals before starting any new physical, emotional, spiritual, or financial practice.

Some sections discuss grief, trauma, and challenging life events and may be emotionally intense. Please take care of yourself as you read, skip what doesn't serve you, and seek support when needed.

Use of this material is at your own discretion and responsibility. If you are in crisis, please call 9-8-8 or 9-1-1.

NOTE ON PRIVACY

To respect the privacy of individuals and places, some names, locations, and identifying details in this book have been changed. While the experiences and reflections shared here are true to my journey, certain elements have been modified to protect the dignity and anonymity of those involved.

For my children, CJ, Carse, Grace

&

Cooper James McCoy 🖤

CONTENTS

INTRODUCTION

Framing

Life is tough. It really is. My grandmother used to say, "This ain't for sissies." While this makes me laugh, it's true.

There are, of course, mountain highs in life, along with the deep, bone-crushing valley lows.

As for me, I want the mountain highs. All the time. Why wouldn't I? Why wouldn't you?

But that's not life. Not reality. Not how it goes.

Still, I believe there are ways to approach life that will lead to more happiness than not. Notice, I didn't say pleasure. Pleasure is a hard night of partying with good friends, doing all the things, laughing your face off. Then, when the next day comes, you're back to the mundane humdrum. Pleasure shakes off pretty quickly.

Happiness, on the other hand, is more like long-burning embers on a sandy beach, or in the mountains. The low-burn fire glows. It warms your hands, your face. The wind catches little flecks of ember, and they sparkle off on wind rivers. Happiness is the slow-burning fire that throws off just enough light to guide you through a dark night. You stare into it, and your mind drops into deeper waters. You melt into the flickers, lost in thought.

As for me, I want happiness, with occasional bursts of pleasure. I'm in this for the long haul. The marathon.

Have you ever seen a painting of a Japanese monk walking with a staff and a small bundle on his back? He's walking the long road, uphill, probably heading to a monastery. That's the energy I'm aiming for in this life.

To live a life of happiness takes reflection, intentionality, and learning. The hard truth is, none of us have enough time in this life to learn all the lessons we need to learn on our own to live a life of happiness. So we must, necessarily, turn to others if we want to crest the learning curve. We must listen and learn from others, and we must pay attention.

Sadly, I lost my father when I was in my mid-twenties. I was a young firefighter and a new husband with a one-year-old son. While I wasn't especially close with my dad at the time, I've missed him terribly ever since. There have been so many moments in life when I've found myself hard-pressed, encircled by jackals, lacking wisdom, and wanting to say, "Dad, what would you do here? What should I do?"

But he's not here to ask. He's not been here for a long time. Many of you can relate.

All things considered, I've done a good job of finding my way in life. The Army National Guard, the fire department, and educational work brought good mentors into my life. Great ones. Some of the best. People I could look up to. People I could ask, "what would you do here, in this situation?"

I learned more about being a father watching Bret Tarver[1] with his family at the fire station than all fatherhood lessons combined. He was such a good dad. I watched, and I learned.

Still, my wisdom has been hard-won and I carry more scars than I should. Some of the scars go past my body and all the way down into my soul. Soul scars.

This book is my attempt at sharing some of my hard-earned wisdom. I wrote it for anyone willing to sit with it, for sure, but if I'm being honest, and I think I should be, I had my sons and daughter in the front of my mind as I wrote this book. This book is for them first and foremost. They are my first loves, with my wife. But it's also for all young men and women finding their way in this world.

This book is also for my students, past, present, and future. I don't want you to get beat up as badly as I have. There's no reason for it. If this book can help you find your footing, even just a little bit, then it's worth it to me to write it. I'm especially thinking of my students at San Miguel High School in Tucson, and my fire science students at Montana State University Billings. I love you and I genuinely miss you. For real.

Of course, you all have your own lives to live and your own experiences to navigate. You will learn many lessons, and some of them, maybe not all, will come the hard way. That's how it goes.

This book is my attempt to walk alongside you in life, even if only in spirit. Consider me your 'third man' who is not going to leave you. If you go, we go.

Consider my words here as a quiet voice on the long road of life.

What You'll Find Inside

Walking alongside you through these pages, I've laid out the wisdom that has helped me navigate my own journey: how to build resilience when life knocks you down, finding mindfulness in a world that never stops moving, balancing honest work with genuine peace, living authentically rather than performing, and recognizing that we need each other – we're better together than alone. These threads weave the fabric of what I call being "grounded" - feet planted firmly on solid earth while keeping an open heart and mind.

This book is yours now. You might read it front to back, or you might find yourself drawn to certain chapters based on what's happening in your life right now. Either approach works. What matters is that you consider returning to "The Work" sections when you need them. Those meditations aren't one-and-done; they're meant to be companions. Pick them up, set them down, and come back to them. They'll be waiting.

Repetition

The first thing you will notice in reading this book is there will be a lot of repetition. Some of the thoughts and ideas I share will be presented several times across chapters, and sometimes even repeated within a chapter. Some of my written reflections will contain similar words, thoughts, phrases, and ideas.

All of this is intentional. I want the repetition. It's on purpose.

We learn by repetition, this is how it is.

Faith

Another consideration as you read concerns Christian faith. I have been a Christian and I have believed. I have also experienced a faith shift in my life and have experimented with different faith-wisdom traditions, to include Buddhism.

Try not to judge me too quickly. Life is hard and you never know how your foundations will be altered.

I want to say this, if you are a Christian, I honor you and support your beliefs. I have no axe to grind and I honor your path. I am not against Jesus. I love Jesus. I have zero regrets about my time spent with Jesus and my many prayers kissed toward heaven. And yet, I trust the love of God to allow me to experience and lean into other traditions that have helped me in time of need in ways that resonated with my life. I mean to say, you are going to see my journey in these pages. You will read how I think of marriage, very Christian, and how I honor meditation.

Keep in mind stages of faith in life and how we progress. I don't believe God is a big, angry male figure, and that I need to follow all the rules or I will burn in hell. I envision God as all loving, most forgiving, and kind to all people. Bear this in mind as you read.

Format

There are 14 chapters in this book, and each chapter follows a predictable rhythm: Situational Awareness, The Work, and Tail-board. I'm using fire service language intentionally because this is the language that has framed so much of my life.

Situational Awareness

In the fire service, and other operational environments, there are three zones: green zone, yellow zone, and red zone.

The green zone is a very relaxed state, like you might feel after eating way too much food at Grandma's house on Thanksgiving

Day. You settle into a chair and before you know it, you're fading. Lights out. This is the green zone.

The yellow zone is where you want to be when you're working on shift at the fire department. Awake. Alert. Prepared. You're humming, your spirit sings, you feel good and look good. You're ready for a 1st Alarm fire to drop. Your game is on.

The red zone is a hyper-alert, highly stressed state. It has its place, like commanding a 3-Alarm fire with occupants trapped, but it's not somewhere you want to stay for long.

Each chapter opens with a short section titled Situational Awareness. I'm asking you to be in the yellow zone as you read it. You're holding a dove in your hands. Not loose, not too tight. Softly, softly, but the hold is present.

Situational Awareness is meant to ease you into the chapter. It's a moment to pause and take stock. You might ask yourself, how does this align with or sit in tension with what follows in The Work and Tailboard?

The Work

The fire department, ultimately, is about the work. The work of protecting life and property in the community, sometimes risking your life in a highly calculated manner to save savable lives.

Firefighters live for the work. It's the work that breathes life into the fire service. The work is where the battle is.

Each chapter includes a second section titled The Work. Like the fireground, this is where the real effort takes place.

I've written The Work in a poetic structure to slow your reading, to invite reflection and attention. Some of the entries are meditations. Some are mantras. Some are field notes. Some ancient.

Read them slowly, let them echo. The Work is the marrow of each chapter.

And I won't give you the answers. That's not my job here. Even if I have my own thoughts on each meditation, I'm not answering them for you.

You have to do the work. Hence, the name.

Tailboard

Learning doesn't happen by accident, not most of the time. We have to be intentional.

In the fire service, after a fire, we conduct a tailboard critique. Firefighters gather at the back of the engine. The battalion chief leads each captain and crew through a few quick questions:

"What did you do upon arrival? How did it go? Would you do anything differently next time?"

The goal is simple. To get better at the craft.

The Tailboard section of each chapter is just that. A longer reflection. A firehouse debrief. A chance to pull up a chair, kick some thoughts around, and tell a story or two. It's where things settle.

Let's go!

At the end of the day, this is a book about living a good life, even if it's a hard one.

You'll encounter a variety of thought and thinking patterns, and this is all intentional.

You'll notice a range of faith-wisdom perspectives, and this too, is on purpose.

Brother. Sister. I am here for you. Yes, you have to live your life on your terms, and I support that.

Just know, like a good firefighter, I'll be with you.

If you go, we go.

Blessings.

———

CHAPTER 1
FOUNDATIONS

SITUATIONAL AWARENESS

When I was a young boy, I wanted to be a doctor. I don't know exactly where the desire to help others came from, but I suspect it had something to do with my father, who served as a Medical Specialist in the U.S. Army.

My parents nurtured my dream to be a doctor. One Christmas, they gave me Grey's Anatomy, the definitive and complete guide to human anatomy and physiology. I spent hours poring over that book looking at the pictures, and years later, I became a fire-fighter-paramedic. As a paramedic in the fire department, I had the opportunity to practice street medicine and save lives in trying situations. I loved it.

When I joined the fire department and when I became a paramedic, I took an oath, standing shoulder to shoulder with my brothers and sisters, swearing to protect life and property in the community and to uphold the Constitution of the United States of America and the Constitution and laws of the State of Arizona.

That oath, to protect life and to do no harm, has been foundational in my life. Foundations matter.

THE WORK

First,

do no harm.[1]

Put your family first

always

every single time.

All people are created equal[2]

period.

There are no chosen people above others.

To thine own self be true.[3]

Between stimulus and response

there is a gap[4]

where we are able to choose

how we respond.

Meditation helps open up this time gap

making it wider.

. . .

Virtue is the means

the middle

between the excesses.[5]

It is balance.

Be virtuous

live virtuously.

The human person is a fusion

of mind, body, and soul.

Your mind, body and soul are

in substantial union

they are one.

What you do with your mind and body

affects your soul

and what happens in the soul

affects the mind and body.

This is why, for example, you cry

physical tears when your soul

is sorrowful.

At death

your soul will separate from your physical body.

Your soul is eternal.

Honesty is the best policy.[6]

The ends never justify the means.
(You cannot use immoral methods to achieve a moral outcome).

Form follows function.[7]
So simple.
Advertisers and marketers focus on form
craftsmen and women focus on function.

Develop a seventh generation mindset.[8]
How are your actions and behaviors today
affecting your family bloodline
seven generations from now?

Breathe.
Begin again
each breath anew
each breath
a fresh start

a new beginning.

Breathe

in through the nose

slowly

deeply

and completely

hold it briefly

let it out the nose

slowly

deeply

and completely.

We are spiritual animals, yes.

But we are also biological

evolved animals.

Evolutionary biology applies to us.

"I am" is a complete sentence.

Our greatest fear as a human

is to be kicked out of the tribe.

. . .

All is grace.[9]

Repeat mantra:

May I be strong and resilient.

or

may I be healthy, happy, safe, and at peace.

Or,

repeat both

repeat often

over and over again.

The deed is all.[10]

What if

it's not all about you?

Chin up

shoulders back

smile.

Let that smile spread across your face.

Turn your beautiful face to the sun

close your eyes

breathe deep

again

smile.

TAILBOARD: OBJECTIVE REALITY

Good morning, friends.

I sit at our new kitchen table, circular, ashen in color, hardwood maple. Quality craftsmanship, built to last.

Yesterday, I ordered a cutting board. I found a hand-crafted piece made in a small, rural woodshop in Pennsylvania. I appreciate that it was made in PA—now that our oldest son lives in Pittsburgh.

Speaking of Pittsburgh, it's a city of working-class folks who shape and mold steel used in structures around the world. These are people who truly understand what it means to work with their hands, crafting materials from wood and steel.

Billings, Montana, where I am currently living and writing from, is the home of miners, railroad workers, oil workers, and farmers and ranchers. A state built on working-class people, those who used the strength of their arms and backs to earn a living for their families.

There's a point to all of this.

All of my life I've been interested in philosophy, reading philo-sophical works and pondering them. Philosophers have long been concerned with cause and effect. Everything comes from some-thing else. It's how St. Thomas Aquinas reasoned, logically, for the existence of God: there must be a First Mover to have set in motion the infinite chain of cause and effect.

Cause and effect also explains karma: our actions today will have downstream consequences, both positive and negative, because of this principle.

But more to the point, philosophers, historically, always worked within the realm of the real world—of reality, of what is objective.

Objective reality is at least what I can touch and feel with my working hands.

This is why research, data, and empirical observation matter. They help us make sense of the objective, real world. This is why investigative journalism, and the journalists who pursue truth, those with a track record of credibility and honest reporting, ought not to be immediately questioned. Follow them. Read them. Be open to truth, rather than closed to it. Not all news is fake news, and there are credible sources and people worth listening to.

Here's where I get concerned: we are now entering a period in the U.S., and perhaps globally, where reality is being distorted. Where truth is questioned. Where people are beginning to not know what is true and what is false.

There is a sense of confusion and chaos. "Fake news." "Post-truth society." These are now common phrases.

Here's the thing: how we come to know the world, to know anything, is through our senses.

This is why people who work with their hands, gardeners, pipefitters, landscapers, woodworkers, craftspeople, mechanics, have a unique and grounded understanding of reality.

Either a nail gets pounded in straight and clean, or it doesn't. There's no fake news about it. The reality feedback loop is immediate.

In rock climbing, you either stick the hold or you don't. There is no faking it.

I recently came across a quote that made me chuckle. It said, jokingly, "Everything outside your smartphone is an illusion."

What I'm arguing is quite the contrary.

Everything outside your phone—rock climbing, gardening, biking, talking with others, cooking food, exercising, is, in fact, reality.

We live in a post-truth society where reality is distorted.

My advice to you is this: Think critically. Use logic. Work with data. Check your sources. Look at who wrote what. What's their background? What's their history of credibility?

Above all, keep working with your hands and your body in the material world.

I am arguing that knowledge of the world is gained through your senses, as you interact with the physical world.

Garden. Climb. Cook. Exercise. Build. Do dishes. Talk to your neighbor. Ride a bike. Make a piece of art. Write a poem.

It is our work with and interaction with the material, objective world, done with purpose and intent, that will keep us grounded as the distortion of reality continues.

Also, strive to spend less time on devices—phones, games, television.

A good example of what happens when people lose their grip on reality? Fringe movements—on both the right and the left—those too willing to resort to violence. People without a strong tether to reality can be more prone to joining these kinds of groups. The distortion of truth has real-world consequences.

In closing, friends, you know I always want the best for each of you. Part of my job is to look out at society with wisdom, to forecast what's happening, and to relay it to you in a way that helps position you for success.

At present, I believe one of the greatest threats we face is this distortion of reality, and the fact that many people do not yet have the mental muscle and critical thinking skills to see it for what it is.

I want you to be better than this.

We are not sheeple. We are Operators. We notice and influence our environments, we shape them, we are not shaped by them.

(Of course, we're always influenced by our environments to some degree. That can't be helped. But we can become more aware of it.)

Be critical in your thinking.

Trust yourself. Trust reason. Trust what you can feel and hold in your hands. Trust empirical evidence. Trust credible sources. Trust research. And trust what you come to know by being outside, by working, by doing.

I think this foundation matters.

———

CHAPTER 2
DAD'S LIST

SITUATIONAL AWARENESS

I moved to Billings, Montana, in January 2017 to begin teaching fire science at Montana State University Billings. My youngest son was a junior in high school in Tucson, Arizona, and we were not going to pull him out of high school just for my job. So, I moved to Montana alone and began commuting back "home" to Tucson every other weekend, flying Allegiant Airlines, Thursday to Sunday. If I was not coming back to Tucson, my family was flying up to Montana to spend time with me.

Living alone, after spending my entire adult life surrounded by family, was hard. Really hard. I kept myself busy, sure, but what truly helped me navigate that season of life was the creation and repetition of a simple mantra.

Every morning in the shower, and anytime I felt the wheels wobbling on the bus, I said my mantra, three times, out loud: May I be strong and resilient.

It's still my go-to mantra. These humble words have carved a path in my mind. When I say them now, my body responds. It lights up. The neurons, they know.

THE WORK

Pray — especially "help" and "thank you"

Breathe

Ground

Meditate

Endure

When you think you're done, you're not

Live in your 3-foot world[1]

Chin up, shoulders back. Smile

Be with family and friends

Win the day

Get 1% better each day[2]

Touch the grass

Repeat mantra: May I be strong and resilient

Take a walk.

TAILBOARD: MINDFULNESS MEDITATION, GROUND, AND KIBBUTZ

Mindfulness Meditation

How did I begin a mindfulness meditation practice? Every journey of a thousand miles begins with one small step. I now have a daily mindfulness meditation practice, and I'm often asked by curious family and friends, "How did you get started?"

It's a fair question, and I think the best way to answer it is by sharing how I found my way in. For context, mindfulness meditation has been shown to increase resilience, and that's what I needed.

Firefighting, my former career, is regularly ranked as one of the most stressful jobs in the world. In 2015, CareerCast ranked firefighting as the most stressful profession, ahead of even Enlisted Military Personnel.[3] Forbes echoed this, citing firefighting as the most stressful job that same year.[4] Multiple studies back this up.

In the general population, about 6.8% of people will experience post-traumatic stress disorder (PTSD) at some point in their lives.[5] Among firefighters, that number jumps to between 5% and 37%.[6] And the longer a firefighter stays on the job, the higher the likelihood of PTSD symptoms. If you're interested, there's a great read called PTSD and Coping Among Career Professional Firefighters.[7]

In other words, firefighting is stressful, and the effects are cumulative. Makes sense, right?

Toward the end of my 25-year career, I began to feel the weight of that accumulated stress. Looking back, I had several symptoms, but the one that stuck out most was anxiety. And if you've experienced anxiety, you know, it sucks.

During the final two weeks of my career, I attended a week-long training called Mindfulness-Based Mind Fitness Training, or "M-Fit."[8] It's designed for people in high-stress operational roles. I went because I needed tools, real tools, to deal with the stress and anxiety that had built up over decades.

Before M-Fit, I had zero experience with mindfulness meditation. But during that week-long intensive, I was introduced to a variety of practices, and afterward, I followed an eight-week home curriculum. I completed it.

That course was the beginning of what is now a daily, non-negotiable mindfulness meditation practice. Since then, I've done other programs and even attended a week-long silent retreat at Spirit Rock: An Insight Meditation Center.

A long, stressful firefighting career brought me to mindfulness. The real, lived results, in my body, in my mind, are what keep me coming back. I can't speak for everyone, but for me, the proof is in the pudding.

Mindfulness meditation has helped regulate my nervous system. It's helped me heal. It has brought a deep sense of calm and clarity that I didn't know I needed until I felt it.

Like any worthy endeavor, it takes effort, patience, and grit. It's not easy to sit quietly with yourself for 20 minutes a day. In a world that never stops moving, stillness can feel like the hardest thing.

But I stayed with it. I meditated even when I didn't feel like it. I made it a priority. I also believe that years of daily prayer and long periods of contemplation primed the pump. They helped ready the soil for this practice to take root.

In closing: beginning a mindfulness practice begins with just that, practice. A commitment to keep showing up. There are hundreds of programs and resources out there. I recommend Mindful Awareness Practices I through the UCLA Mindful Awareness Research Center.[9] It's online, it's research-based, and it's a solid place to begin.

Most importantly: listen to yourself. Care for yourself. Beginning a daily mindfulness meditation practice might be the best decision you ever make.

It was for me.

Ground

Morning, friends. I hope you survived your evening. Remember, menudo is the cure-all soup for hangovers. Find a local Mexican joint and be healed.

Well, I survived my first professional development training. It wasn't terrible. I still maintain that hypersensitivity to "identities" is going to backfire and actually deepen our divisions. I fall back on what I learned in Catholic graduate school, that every person has moral worth and a soul, and is therefore worthy of dignity and respect. All people carry that which is 'of God' within them. Seems simpler to me.

I believe we live in an objective world. Things exist outside of our minds. Whether I like it or not, whether I want it to be true or not, I am here, on a planet, on a piece of land, with family, friends, and pets. If I were to die tomorrow and take my mind with me, the planet would keep spinning. The land, the people, the dogs, they'd still be here.

Most of you were handed smartphones around age 13. You were given access to a kind of reality that isn't real. A world not physically tangible, but existing in bandwidth and data packets beamed through the "cloud." You've grown up in fantasy games and social media feeds that have substituted for real, physical relationships.

As someone whose brain wasn't shaped by tech, I've noticed that you all struggle with this: "what's real and what's simulation?" I don't think it's your fault, but I do believe, as someone once said, that "technology is not morally neutral."

So here's the thing: you must be intentional about staying grounded, staying connected to the physical world, probably for the rest of your lives.

When I was working through my own PTSD, my mind often took me to places that weren't real, but felt real. My healing started with a concept called grounding. Staying present. Coming back to the real world.

Meditation helped. It trained me to notice the moment: the sights, the sounds, the smells, the sensations. It kept me here, instead of floating off into anxiety loops.

I swam a lot during that time, laps at the country club in the quiet evenings. The physicality of swimming, the feel of water moving over my body, the effort required to push through it, that grounded me.

I hiked. I cooked. I did yard work. I barely touched my phone. My wife got mad because I never carried it with me. I walked the dogs. I hung out with the puppies. I got back into my body and into the world.

What I'm telling you is this: if you continue on your current path, you will continue to struggle with anxiety, depression, and disconnection from reality. Why? Because tech has outpaced biology. Your brains are wired to scan for mountain lions, and you're feeding them 1,000 lions a day via stimulus.

Your synapses are overloaded. Your dopamine system is shot. You are fried, and you're too young to be fried.

Let me put it plainly. After 25 years in a busy fire department system, my nervous system was cooked. The repeated hits of adrenaline from emergency calls had worn my body down.

You may not be running into burning buildings, but you're dosing your brain every day, dopamine hits, fear spikes, comparison loops. Again and again.

Never in human history has a generation of 15- to 25-year-olds experienced this level of anxiety, despair, and detachment from the real.

You know it's true.

So here's my advice: Accept that technology is not neutral. And accept that too much of it will break you. Once you concede that, then it's time to act.

The cure? Ground.

Swim. Meditate. Box. Wrestle. Cook. Garden. Hike. Hunt. Fish. Rock climb. Walk the dogs. Build something. Wash your car. Share meals without phones. Have a drink with your friends, no phones. Read a real book. Throw axes. Do yard work. Birdwatch. Snow ski. Lift weights. Move your body.

Get grounded. Get back in touch with what's real.

I believe, truly, that the greatest threat to your future and your health is your smartphone. It's more addictive than crack and opium combined. You're not holding the phone; the phone is holding you.

But when you're grounded, you can see clearly. You develop the ability to parse through the noise and the nonsense. You gain a leg up in life, standing on the mountain, watching the landscape unfold, while others are down in the weeds, spinning in circles.

So here's my ask: make a resolution. Do more in the physical world. Use less technology. Be active, be present, be aware. You harm yourself if you don't.

Put the phone down. Pick up something real. Work with your hands.

This is the path to happiness.

Ground.

Kibbutz

Years ago, I visited Israel while on a delegation with Firefighters Without Borders. While the trip brought the usual highlights— Jerusalem, Tel Aviv, the Mediterranean coastline—I also worked off the beaten path and was able to spend time with Israel Fire & Rescue and the Israel Defense Force Home Front Command's fire-fighters. But what stayed with me most wasn't the cities or the monuments. It wasn't the fire and rescue training. It was an after-noon I spent on a kibbutz: Yad Mordechai.

At the time, I wasn't thinking about "mindfulness" or "grounding." I didn't yet have a daily meditation practice. I wasn't using words like resilience or intentional living. But I see it now. Many of the values I've come to hold close were lived out in quiet, tangible ways on that land.

The kibbutz was green. It was quiet. There was rhythm and order, but not the kind that felt rigid—more like a shared agreement on how to live well, together. I remember the people being strong, steady, not of many words. It reminded me of the farmers I'd met in the Midwest. They just worked. There was something sacred in the way they moved through their days.

One thing that struck me was how the children lived communally, raised not only by their parents but also by trusted caretakers. Parents still saw them each afternoon, but the time was focused, present, undistracted. Three to four hours a day of true togetherness. It made me think: how many hours do we actually spend with our kids, undistracted by screens or work or the noise of modern life?

The kibbutz also had a deeper logic. Strategically located, it served both agricultural and geopolitical purposes—helping feed the country, yes, but also defining the borders of Israel and standing as a first barrier to outside aggression. These weren't abstract ideals. They were boots-on-the-ground realities. Cultivate the land. Protect the land. Share what you grow. Take care of one another.

Even now, years later, I still think about that visit. Something about it stuck with me. I didn't name it at the time, but what I saw there was a kind of grounded living. Not theoretical. Not idealized. Just slow, simple, real.

Today, when I talk about "touch the grass," or "ground," or "be with family," this is part of what I'm trying to name. The way we live matters. The pace, the presence, the priority of people over things —it matters. And while we don't live on kibbutzim, we can still choose how we build our rhythms and spend our days.

If I go back to Israel, I won't beeline to Jerusalem or Tel Aviv. I'll visit another kibbutz. I'll walk the land. I'll listen again to the silence, to the sound of work being done with purpose. There's something grounded and holy there. I want more of it in my life.

―――

CHAPTER 3
LIFE

SITUATIONAL AWARENESS

I didn't have much direction in high school. I had the aptitude, but not the right academic attitude. School evaded me. What I really wanted was to be out there, doing something with my body—most especially, snow skiing.

After graduation, I enrolled at the local community college without much of a plan. I ended up taking a course in Emergency Medical Technology (EMT), thinking it might help me land a job as a ski patroller at Sunrise Ski Resort in Arizona.

The EMT course was taught by two fire captains from the local fire department. Their stories, their presence—it hooked me. I started to take an interest in firefighting. In fact, as the course wrapped up, I applied to the Fire Department and even landed an interview.

Still, I wanted that job on the mountain. I interviewed with the Director of Ski Patrol at Sunrise. The personal interview was on the chairlift going up, and the practical interview was burning turns on the way down. I was offered the job.

When I got home, I found out the fire department wanted to hire me too.

I had a decision to make: ski patroller or firefighter. A real fork in the road.

I chose the fire department, and that decision has shaped the course of my life ever since.

THE WORK

Apply strategy to life.

He that gives

too much

is better than he

who is a miser.[1]

Creator, this land and these fields

all belong to You.

Bring the sun, bring the rain

and keep the predators from our fields.

There are two kinds of pain in this world:

the pain that hurts

and the pain that alters.[2]

. . .

Good soup will wake the dead.[3]

Reading is the key

Live and let live

Live, love, and learn.[4]

88% of life is showing up.[5]

Solvitur ambulando —

it is solved by walking.

Where am I? I'm right here.

What time is it? It is right now.

Smile and don't take yourself too seriously.

Be like a postage stamp

stick to one thing until you get there.

Breathe

chin up, shoulders back

stand tall

smile

you got this.

Garbage in garbage out

GIGO.[6]

Walk softly and carry a big stick.[7]

Give a man a fish you feed him for a day.

Teach a man to fish you feed him for a lifetime.

Be a teacher.

Take highly calculated risks sometimes.

No stinking thinking.[8]

Begin with the end in mind.[9]

Keep good situational awareness (SA).

Never never never give up.[10]

. . .

If you need to go pro, go pro.

See a doctor, counselor, attorney, coach.

Never hit a girl. Ever.

Learn a foreign language

Learn to play a musical instrument

Learn.

Your best effort is always good enough.

Dream big

always follow your dreams.

A ship in harbor is safe

but eventually its bottom will rot out.

Hit the high seas.[11]

Surround yourself with great people

be humble.

Behind every successful person is a great partner.

. . .

Have fun

be careful

stay safe.

Breathe.

It's the cracked ones

who let light into the world.

True.

Two questions to ask:

Are you happy where you are?

Are you happy doing what you're doing?[12]

Life is choice management

good choices beget good choices.

Karma?

Say "please," "thank you," and "you're welcome."

Sufficient are the worries of this day.[13]

. . .

If you get on the wrong train

get off at the nearest station

the longer you ride

the more expensive the return.[14]

Snitches get stitches.[15]

Loose lips sink ships.

Measure twice cut once.[16]

Have a bucket list.

A bird in hand is worth two in the bush.

Be on time.

Learn to be comfortable being uncomfortable

this is hard

very hard.

Watch the sunrise.

. . .

If you have built castles in the air,

your work need not be lost —

that is where they should be.

Now, put the foundations under them.[17]

Put your hands up on the 808 bump.[18]

Smile, breathe, pray

walk in the sun

smell the flowers

garden, cook

tinker

read good books by dead authors

buy the brown eggs

eat, drink, be merry.

Reminders for hard days:

A bad day does not equal a bad life

Not all thoughts are true

Feelings aren't facts — but all feelings are valid

The only way out is through

Your worth isn't contingent

Nothing stays the same

You can't be everything to everyone

Be gentle. Trust your voice

You're not alone

Focus on what you can control

Source: Wholehearted School Counseling[19]

It's OK to cry

tears are healing.

Put your bare feet in the grass, in the sand.

The only thing necessary for the triumph of evil

is that good people do nothing.[20]

Read The Old Man and the Sea

Watch On Golden Pond

Objective reality

Objective moral truth

Two solid pillars.

. . .

The pen is mightier than the sword.[21]

Hard work beats talent

when talent doesn't work hard.

The strength of the pack is the wolf

and the strength of the wolf is the pack.[22]

Do you have a bug-out bag?

The prepper mentality: one is none, two is one.

Square this with minimalism and an abundance mindset.

A vision:

to age gracefully

not fear death

live long, healthy, happy

die of natural causes

surrounded by love.

Each day:

Walk 45 minutes

Read 30 minutes

Meditate and pray 20 minutes

Win the day.

Take a gap year

why not?

Centenarians say:

take more risk

have fewer regrets.

Individualism vs. collectivism

we carry both impulses.

Paradox: self-reliance is formed in community.

Mama never told me there'd be days like this.

They will pass.

Let's be honest

change is hard.

PMA: Positive Mental Attitude

have one.

Box breathing
learn it, know it, practice.

No man is self-made
do hard things.
find good work for your hands
and another to love.

We never step into the same stream twice.

Know your why.
He who has a why to live for
can bear almost any how.[23]

A 1,000-mile journey begins with one step.[24]

Sometimes the juice is not worth the squeeze.

"Men wanted for hazardous journey.
Low wages, Bitter cold,

Long hours of complete darkness.

Safe return doubtful.

Honor and recognition in the event of success."[25]

Two in, two out

we work in pairs.

Never leave your wingman

we don't leave fallen comrades behind[26]

if you go, we go.[27]

Put fresh herbs in your eggs.

Practice deferred gratification.

Set goals

Chart your course

Take the step.

Be strong

Be stoic

Be lions.

. . .

Sometimes the grass is greener on the other side

sometimes not.

"All of humanity's problems stem from man's

inability to sit quietly in a room alone."[28]

Try it

no phone, no music, no book

one hour alone

one room and you.

Buy real wood furniture.

Be critical

trust logic, facts, experience.

Get your hands dirty.

History doesn't repeat but it echoes.[29]

Nature or nurture?

Both shape us.

Work with your hands

learn a trade

even if just for you.

Travel

see New Zealand, Nepal.

Take the long view

seven generations.[30]

God, family, country

not (entirely) off the mark.

Most people are battling something.

Don't be a tool of the man

f the man.[31]

Be free.

. . .

Say your mantra often:

"May I be strong and resilient."

Stay the course

Do good.

Push good into the world

Breathe

Live your best life.

TAILBOARD: JV DEATH REFLECTION

I was once a young firefighter on a busy engine company in a suburban fire department. Our station was a multi-company house with an engine, a ladder truck, and a two-person battalion chief vehicle. Ten firefighters on shift. At that time, across all three shifts—A, B, and C—100% of the firefighters were men.

Working at big firehouses was always fun for me. There was never a dull moment. With ten firefighters together for 24 hours, the station was full of activity and camaraderie.

Here's something you may not know about fire stations: they are largely self-governed. The crews, the tools, the equipment—we managed it all. It's a powerful example of decentralized leadership. We knew the mission, and we did the work.

The kitchen table in a fire station is sacred space. At our station, and many others around the world, every day we gathered around the table for lunch and dinner. We talked, laughed, remembered calls. After dinner, we'd clean the kitchen, mop the floors, and head outside to chew tobacco and swap stories.

Most of us had families. We loved our families and talked about them often. We also, of course, whined and complained about them too. That's real life.

One morning, I walked into the station ready to start my shift. As usual, I went straight to the kitchen table to catch up with the off-going crew. That informal exchange at the table was part of our ritual—passing the torch.

But this morning, something was different. The men around the table were quiet, heavy, somber. I walked in joking, "What's up with you all? Did somebody die?"

Not quite. But close.

JV, a firefighter on B-shift, had a seizure the day before during equipment checks. He was in the apparatus bay, checking the power saws on the ladder truck, when his captain looked over and saw him on the ground, seizing.

He was rushed to the hospital and diagnosed with a brain tumor. JV was in his mid-twenties. The tumor was inoperable, though radiation could shrink it.

That meant he was going to die—not right away, but in time.

He had a wife. A beautiful little girl. Their daughter would later be a student in my wife's class at the local public school.

Time passed. JV returned to work. At that point, I didn't know how long he had. We didn't talk about it much.

About a year later, I walked into the firehouse again and saw the same somber faces. The kitchen table said it all.

JV was back in the hospital. The tumor had returned. This time with force.

That morning, JV had woken up and knew. He just knew. He kissed his wife. He kissed his sleeping daughter. He got into his old Ford pickup—a working man's truck—and drove himself across town to the Neurological Institute.

To die.

My crew and I loaded into the engine and drove to the hospital. JV lay unconscious in his bed, still alive.

I walked to his bedside, took his hand, and told him I loved him. I told him we would do our best to care for his family. That I hoped to see him again in heaven.

His body writhed slightly, tensed. He didn't wake up. But I believe he heard me.

I walked out of the room in tears. JV died later that day.

The reason this story has stayed with me so deeply is because of what JV showed us that day:

Courage.

He didn't panic. He didn't complain. He accepted reality. He began with the end in mind. He stayed the course. He did the next right thing.

This is what courage looks like. This is what manhood looks like.

In our current moment, where men are often criticized or confused about their place in society, JV stood tall. He showed us the way.

When I've faced hard things in my life, I've remembered JV. If he could stare death in the face and walk into it with that kind of resolve, then surely I can face whatever life throws at me.

You each have your own lives, your own stories. But I wish I could sit with you around that kitchen table. I wish you could smell the fire station, feel the hum of the shift, understand how deeply that space holds both humor and heartbreak.

That morning with JV is etched into my soul.

Watch the sunrise. Be strong. Be stoic. Be lions. Live long. Be healthy. Be happy. Die surrounded by love.

May we all be like JV. May we all have the courage to face life—and death—with honor.

Rest in peace, JV.

———

CHAPTER 4
RELATIONSHIPS

SITUATIONAL AWARENESS

A few months ago, I had dinner and a couple beers with my cousin in Bozeman, Montana. We got to talking about the meaning of life. She told me she believes it's this: to celebrate with family and friends. Not getting wasted, but taking time to honor the moments worth celebrating.

A home-cooked meal with people you love? That's a celebration. New Year's at grandma's house? Celebration. Laughing with friends on a back porch somewhere? Celebration.

We shouldn't overlook these simple moments with the people we love. These are the moments that make life worth living.

The Book of Ecclesiastes says that to have good work for your hands, someone to love, and to eat, drink, and be merry, that's the best we can hope for in this life. I believe that.

One of my fondest memories from my time overseas was staying with a host family for a night—a mom and dad with five kids, only one still living at home. They lived near the border, where tensions were high, and yet they carried this calm, grounded energy.

They grew herbs in the yard. They fed us a homemade meal. They smiled easily, talked with kindness, poured us wine. They found peace in the small movements of the soul: growing food, tending to their space, welcoming strangers.

In the middle of a storm, they chose peace. And celebration.

THE WORK

Love equals time

Love = presence, action, and time

Love is a verb, an action.

It should be observable.

Families with dogs are happier families

happy is the man who has his quiver full of children.[1]

Read to your children

Call your mom, often

Text your mom, often

Honor your parents

(It is one of the Ten Commandments)

Your mother,

including Mother Mary and Mother Kuan Yin

always knows best

always love her.

Nobody in this world loves you more

than your mom

your siblings

and your dad.

Women love to talk and to be heard.

Listen to them.

Learn to listen and to hear a woman.

Women do love flowers.

Discover your wife's emotional needs

or her primary love language

and work to meet her needs

and to speak her love language.

Note: Her needs and love language

are likely different than yours.

Watch how boys treat their mothers

it tells you how they might treat their future wife[2]

The way a boy honors his mother

reveals the man he will become.

. . .

Mothers teach sons how to love women.

Marriage is a lifelong commitment

It is a vow

Vows can't be undone

Marriage is God's idea

Commitment is essential

Romance is important

Marriage holds times of great joy

Marriage creates the best environment for raising children.

Marriage is permanent and eternal

you can't undo it.

Ideally only death should dissolve a marriage.

Marriage is based on the principal practice of love

not on feelings.

Marriage is a living symbol of Christ and his Church.[3]

Marriage is good and honorable.

Unfaithfulness breaks the bonds of trust

the foundation of all relationships.

Trust is the foundation of all relationships.

DWYSYWD = Do what you say you will do.

This builds trust.

If you're ever having relationship problems

don't leave your bed.

A fire department chaplain gave me this advice:

First you leave your bed

then you leave the house

then you leave your marriage.[4]

I used this advice when going through significant marital challenges

and it likely saved our marriage.

All marriages will have bad days, yes

and most marriages will have bad years.

Most couples who commit to stay in their relationship

and work through their problems

will be happy again.

The divorce rate for second marriages is very high, near 70%.

I think my marriage has been good

because we are aligned on the big values:

children

pets

education

travel

religion

money

and politics.

Birds of a feather flock together.

But also

opposites attract.

Enjoy good meals with family and friends.

Eat slowly.

Family gatherings and celebrations

honor them.

In our home:

We do second chances

We do grace

We do real

We do mistakes

We do "I'm sorry"

We do loud, really well

We do hugs

We do family

We do love.[5]

Stay connected to family and friends

Keep in touch, always

Give of yourself to others

Find your tribe

Paradox: Self-reliance is found in community.

Jesus sent his disciples out two by two.[6]

There is safety in others.

There is safety in numbers.

Never leave your wingman.

Go out together

stay together.

"If you go, we go."[7]

TAILBOARD: ROAD TRIP

In the coming months, I will have the opportunity to go on a three-day road trip with my oldest son. We are helping a friend move across the country and they need help moving one of their cars. With the help of my son, we are going to drive for three days and spend quality father-son time together. I think it's going to be amazing.

This little road trip has got me thinking about something that's been on my mind for many years. The practicalities of life have pushed it aside, but the dream clings by its fingernails to hope that one day it will manifest in reality.

The first dream I have is to take my children on a road trip in an RV to Silver Strand State Beach, California, and camp for a week. The simple rule that I would require is no smartphones. I envision days on the beach, body surfing, stand-up paddle boarding, surfing, fishing, campfires, laughter, sun, sand, and smiles. At night, we meet our friendly neighbors and enjoy fellowship with salt riding the wind around us. There's nothing like the beach.

Secondly, I dream of taking one of my kids across country in a VW Bus. In my dream, we buy an old VW many months before the road trip. We spend evenings, or some evenings, in the garage, working together on fine-tuning our purchase. We make our old VW seaworthy, and get her ready for a cross-country road trip. This working on the VW in the garage with my kid is mostly quiet time, but we do have primitive conversations—the kind of conversations that only fathers and sons, or daughters, can know.

Then, for two months over the forthcoming summer, we drive our VW Bus across the country, stopping along the way to see sights and visit friends and dine in mom-and-pop diners. It's a slow, mindful road trip that strengthens deep bonds between a father and his child.

When we get across the coast, we sell the Bus and fly home, toasting to a memory that lives in eternity.

And sometimes, the dream gets to live itself out.

I recently had the opportunity to go on a four-day road trip with my oldest son, CJ. We drove from Tempe, Arizona to Pismo Beach, California, then up the coast on PCH 1 to Monterey, and on to Portland, Oregon. Once we hit Portland, we stayed one day and night and then flew home via Southwest Airlines.

I love my children, all of them, and I love spending time with them. As my children age, it has become more difficult to spend quality time together, especially one-on-one. They are busy with school, social lives, and building their futures. It's all good, but when I can, I jump at the opportunity to "go" and road trip with them.

My friend, an exceptional and visionary general practitioner, was moving from Tucson to Portland to practice medicine. He needed help moving one of his cars. Rather than pay a moving company, I offered to drive it if he would cover lodging, per diem, and travel home. In the end, I was able to help my friend and his family and enjoy a road trip with my son. Win-win.

Day 1 Tempe to Pismo Beach, 560 miles, 8.5 hours. We hit the road at 6 a.m., had lunch near San Bernardino, and made it to our hotel by 3 p.m. We stayed at the SeaCrest Oceanfront Hotel. Upon arrival, the front desk gave us a bottle of Happy Camper Chardonnay and two glasses.

Up in our room, fourth floor, we stood on the balcony over-looking the Pacific Ocean and toasted our time together. It was the first glass of wine I've ever shared with my son. It was special.

Later, we walked the beach to the Pismo Pier, watched locals fishing, wandered shops, and landed at Papi's Grill for tacos. Papi's kills it. They only serve tacos, twenty kinds, and they were excellent. As one of my sons would say, "it was beast." Sitting at Papi's, with a cold Corona, the sea in our noses, tacos in hand, that was a moment I'll cherish a long time.

Day 2 Breakfast on the patio, firepit nearby, ocean in front. Peaceful silence. Then north, up Pacific Coast Highway 1, through Big Sur, one of the most iconic drives in the world. It's 144 miles from San Luis Obispo to Carmel, a National Scenic Byway.

It was incredible. We lost all cell and radio coverage. My son plugged in his phone and U2's California started to play. Perfect.

We stopped often, breathed in the coastline, visited the elephant seals at Piedras Blancas, had lunch in Carmel, and prepped for a long drive ahead.

From Woodland, California to Portland, it rained the entire way. Snow and sleet at Mount Shasta, fog in Oregon. We missed our hotel in Cottage Grove by an hour and a half, didn't turn back. Landed at a Holiday Inn in Wilsonville at 1 a.m. Seventeen hours of driving. I now know all the top 40 songs, including Adele's Hello—we heard it at least thirty times.

Day 3 Late check-out, slow morning. Into downtown Portland. I'm a fan of Portlandia the show, and now I was in the real thing. It delivered. Portland is weird, smart, defiant, and alive.

We walked, browsed, and lunched at Noodles & Company. Pad Thai and a local ale for me. Then, Powell's City of Books. A place I've always wanted to visit. My son and I split up for a few hours— he wandered downtown while I wandered Powell's.

That night we met up with Lo, my friend's wife. Delivered the car. Toured their new home. Dinner at Cheesecake Factory. A quiet night.

Day 4 Morning coffee and conversation with Lo, life talk. Then errands, breakfast at Denny's, and a final stop: Voodoo Doughnut.

We were serenaded by the workers, probably cursed too, and I brought a half-dozen home to the tribe.

Then airport, through LA, and home.

Closing Time, in my estimation, is more precious than money. While I may have retired young in the eyes of our consumer-driven culture, and basically cut my salary in half, I now have time in abundance. And I am able to do road trips with my children on the spur of the moment, something I otherwise could not do.

I had four days alone with my oldest son. We broke bread, raised a toast, traveled an iconic road, and met Portland... together.

I bought my son On the Road by Jack Kerouac at Powell's and inscribed the opening page with highlights from our journey.

And maybe we didn't restore a VW bus. Maybe we didn't surf Silver Strand. But we built something better than a vehicle—we built memory.

And that memory, I hope, will last him forever.

CHAPTER 5
FAITH & WISDOM

SITUATIONAL AWARENESS

Though I spent 25 years in the fire service, working my way up from firefighter, paramedic, captain, battalion chief, to division chief, I've always considered myself an educator at heart. When I retired from the fire department, I became a freshman religious studies teacher at a small, private Catholic high school.

Part of my job was to teach the Sacraments. In the Roman Catholic tradition, Sacraments are visible signs of invisible grace, symbols of something deeper happening beneath the surface. One day, I was teaching on the Sacrament of Anointing of the Sick. It's a healing Sacrament, and when possible, it's also the one given before death.

As I was teaching, one of the students in class, RG, raised her hand. She began to tell us a story about her grandmother, who had recently passed. They'd been very close.

RG walked us through it, what it looked and felt like to witness the Sacrament in real time. The priest arriving at her grandmother's bedside. The oil. The smell of the fragrance. The prayers. Her grandmother's response.

By the time RG finished, there wasn't a dry eye in the room. Twenty-nine students and one teacher, wrecked.

When I left San Miguel High School to take a teaching position in Montana, RG gave me her grandmother's worn crucifix necklace. She wanted me to have it. I still have that necklace. It's the greatest gift I've ever been given.

THE WORK

The smallest indivisible unit in the Kingdom of God

is two

not one.[1]

Everyone

everyone

every single one

has that of which is God within them.[2]

Chop wood and carry water

before enlightenment and after.

Then Mary said

"Behold the maidservant of the Lord

let it be to me according to your word."[3]

God is the breath within the breath.

Breathe

in through the nose

slowly

deeply

and completely

hold it briefly

let it out the nose

slowly

deeply

and completely.

And Jesus increased in wisdom and stature

and in favor with God and man.[4]

Pure and undefiled religion before God the Father is this:

To look after orphans and widows in their distress

and to keep oneself unpolluted from the world.[5]

. . .

Be quiet

tame your tongue.[6]

For by grace you have been saved.[7]

Aspire to lead a quiet life

to mind your own business

and to work with your hands.[8]

Be strong and courageous.[9]

As for me and my house

we will serve the Lord.[10]

God, grant me the serenity

to accept the things I cannot change

courage to change the things I can

and the wisdom to know the difference.[11]

"Some want to live within the sound

Of church or chapel bell;

I want to run a rescue shop,

Within a yard of hell."[12]

God has shown you what is good

and what He requires of you:

Be just

Love mercy

Walk humbly with your God.[13]

"I know the plans I have for you," declares the Lord—

"plans to prosper you and not to harm you,

plans to give you hope and a future."[14]

Breaking bread around the kitchen table is sacred time.

No television, no phones

look each other in the eyes, talk and listen.

Don't judge a man until you've walked a mile in his shoes.

Judge not, lest you be judged.[15]

Don't look at the speck in your brother's eye

when you have a plank in your own.[16]

. . .

Read the Bible

especially the Psalms

and Gospels:

Matthew, Mark, Luke, and John.

Consider belief

Consider trust

Consider a relationship with Jesus Christ.

Pray often

even if "thank you" and "help"

are the only prayers you can get out.

The Golden Rule, found in all faith-wisdom traditions:

Do unto others as you would have them do unto you.

Forgive.

You are forgiven.

Love your neighbor

(easier said than done).

. . .

Practice the Greatest Commandment:

Love God with all your heart, soul, mind, and strength

and love your neighbor as yourself.[17]

Always help those less fortunate.

Treat others, especially the downtrodden

with kindness, dignity, and respect.

Take your children to church

to the sangha

to Mosque

to the Meeting.

But take them to worship.

Attend church, meeting, or meditation

not out of duty

but out of love.

You only have one mother and one father

honor them.

. . .

You are the captain of your ship

the master of your fate.

God gave you free will

you do have the ability to choose right from wrong.

Breathe and focus.

Agape: Deep, unconditional love. A choice.

Follow your bliss.

Jump and the net will appear.

The Ten Commandments:[18]

No other gods before Me

Do not worship idols

Do not take the Lord's name in vain

Honor the Sabbath

Honor your mother and father

You shall not murder

You shall not commit adultery (Not even in your heart)

You shall not steal

Do not lie

Do not covet your neighbor's things, or their spouse.

For God so loved the world

that He gave His only begotten Son

that whosoever believes in Him

shall not perish

but have everlasting life.[19]

Hail, Mary, full of grace

the Lord is with thee

Blessed art thou among women

and blessed is the fruit of thy womb, Jesus

Holy Mary, Mother of God

pray for us sinners

now and at the hour of our death

Amen.[20]

Take time, perhaps a year

to practice and understand prayer

not rushed prayer

Deep prayer.

Experiment with many different practices and forms

find what works

commit to a lifetime of prayer.

The Golden Rule again:

Do to others as you would have them do to you

a foundational moral truth across all major religions.

Our Father, who art in heaven

hallowed be Thy name

Thy kingdom come

Thy will be done

on earth as it is in heaven

give us this day our daily bread

and forgive us our trespasses

as we forgive those who trespass against us

lead us not into temptation, but deliver us from evil

Amen.[21]

Cardinal Virtues:[22] the "center" of the heart

There are four:

Prudence: Practical wisdom, to discern good and choose it

Justice: The firm will to give their due to God and neighbor

Fortitude: Courage, endurance, constancy in the pursuit of good

Temperance: Moderation in pleasures; balance.

Cardinal virtues point toward character and destiny.

Read Ecclesiastes

there is nothing new under the sun

to everything, a season.

Nothing is better than to rejoice and do good in life

to eat and drink and enjoy the good of all labor

it is the gift of God.

Walk prudently into the house of God

draw near to listen

do not be rash with your mouth

let your words be few

fear God.

Go eat your bread with joy

drink your wine with a merry heart

live joyfully with the one you love.

Whatever your hand finds to do

do it with all your might.

Words of the wise, spoken quietly

should be heard rather than the shout of a ruler of fools.

Wisdom is better than weapons of war.

Do not leave your post.

Of making many books there is no end

and much study wearies the flesh.

If someone inspires you to walk a mile with them

walk two.[23]

Psalm 23

The Lord is my shepherd; I shall not want

He makes me lie down in green pastures

He leads me beside the still waters

He restores my soul

He leads me in the paths of righteousness

for His name's sake.

Yea, though I walk through the valley of the shadow of death

I will fear no evil

for You are with me

Your rod and Your staff, they comfort me.

You prepare a table before me in the presence of my enemies

You anoint my head with oil

my cup runs over.

Surely goodness and mercy shall follow me

all the days of my life

and I will dwell in the house of the Lord

forever.[24]

Those who wait on the Lord shall renew their strength.

They shall mount up with wings like eagles

they shall run and not be weary

they shall walk and not faint.[25]

Benaiah chased a lion into a pit on a snowy day and killed it.[26]

We all have a lion to face

do you have the courage and faith

to get into the pit with yours?

Read and reflect on the Parable of the Good Samaritan.[27]

. . .

Faith is a journey

Give yourself time

Make space to reflect

Let God draw you closer

Everyone's faith journey is different

Be open

Journal

Read scripture and other wisdom

Pray

Gather

Risk the journey.

Karma is cause and effect

what you do and think today shapes your tomorrow

you reap what you sow.

Buddhism Five Precepts:

Protect all life

Take only what is offered

Express sexual energy wisely

Speak truth and kindness

Do not cloud the mind with intoxicants

Eightfold Path:

Wise view

Wise intention

Wise speech

Wise action

Wise livelihood

Wise effort

Wise mindfulness

Wise concentration

Four Noble Truths:[28]

There is suffering

We suffer because we cling

We don't have to suffer

The Eightfold Path leads to liberation

Researchers once visited Buddhist monks

and wired their heads with electrodes

the monks laughed.

When asked why

they said the mind is not in the head

it's in the body.

Metta: Sending loving-kindness.

"May Carse be happy and at peace today."

The kitchen table is sacred space.

The Divine usually shows up in the mundane

learn to see God in the little things.

The Five Pillars of Islam:

Shahada: Declaration of faith

There is no god but Allah

and Muhammad is His messenger.

Salat: Five daily prayers

Dawn, noon, afternoon, sunset, night

Facing Mecca with devotion.

Zakat: Obligatory charity

Give from your wealth to those in need

Purify what you possess.

Sawm: The holy fast of Ramadan

From dawn until sunset

Abstain to purify the soul.

Hajj: Pilgrimage to Mecca

Once in life if able

Journey to the sacred House.[29]

"The great sins, so the Sherpas say,

are to pick wildflowers

and to threaten children."[30]

Sherpa wisdom comes from footsteps on stone

and breath at the edge of the world.

"The mountains are not stadiums

where I satisfy my ambition to achieve

they are the cathedrals

where I practice my religion."[31]

Slowly, slowly

(bistari, bistari)

Not a climbing principle

a Sherpa way of life.

. . .

Before climbing, a good climber must pray.

Then on the mountain

you should not be attached to reaching the summit

or afraid of falling.

Better to return ten times

than to perish once.

Sherpa values:

Community above individualism

Stillness over speed

Reverence for the land and ancestors

Resilience through hardship

Generosity to strangers

Presence in small acts

Sherpas do not "scale" Everest

They journey with it

after asking permission.

All people carry the divine within.

Namaste:[32]

The God in me sees the God in you.

Shortest sentence in the Bible:

Jesus wept.[33]

Look at the birds of the air

they neither toil nor spin

yet your heavenly Father feeds them

Are you not of more value than they?[34]

How beautiful a day can be when love touches it.[35]

Pursue truth

beauty

and goodness.

Smell the flowers.

What is the sound of peace?

What are the sounds of peace?

Listen.

. . .

Hear the children playing
amazing Grace.

You do have a guardian angel
we all do.

Lord Jesus Christ
have mercy on me
a sinner.[36]

The creation waits in eager expectation
for the sons and daughters of God
to reveal themselves.[37]

On the Sabbath, Saturday
do nothing but rest
if not Saturday, find another day.
The point: One day each week rest.

To see a World in a Grain of Sand,
And a Heaven in a Wild Flower,

Hold Infinity in the palm of your hand,

And Eternity in an hour.[38]

Prayer:

Om Mani Padme Hum[39]

Three great questions of existence:

Where did I come from?

Why am I here?

Where am I going (when I die)?

No God but God.[40]

TAILBOARD: METAPHYSICS

Metaphysics is a very good starting point for considering life.

"Meta" means above, and "physics" means nature. Metaphysics therefore means "above nature." Metaphysics considers what is beyond the natural, physical world we live in, the spiritual realm of things, things not found in the natural world. Metaphysics considers the three big questions humans have asked themselves since the beginning of time:

1. Where did I come from?
2. What am I doing here?
3. Where am I going when I die?

I can't tell a person what to believe nor what they should found their life upon. Metaphysical truth must be arrived at through personal trial and error and life experience. I do think it is important, though, to believe that there is something more to life than our life on Earth. If we are only products of evolutionary biology and random chance, then this seems rather depressing to me. Don't get me wrong, it's clear that evolution is taking place, but I still believe it's within a larger spiritual framework of the universe. Take Aristotle's Forms or the Greek Logos, for example.

Life is a journey, and any understanding of truth will likely change with time. One should never be too hard on themselves if they experience a faith/wisdom (metaphysical) shift during the course of their life. For example, if one were once a Christian and then later becomes a Buddhist or an agnostic, it's okay. This is the journey. A thousand-mile journey begins with the first step.

This said, let me share where I have been and where I am at in my metaphysical journey.

I was not raised as overtly religious by my parents. My mom dragged me to church by my ears on a few occasions, the Methodist church, but our attendance was spotty at best. My father claimed to believe in God when I was a child, but he didn't profess a Christian faith. His family was Lutheran.

When I was 25 years of age, my wife, Victoria, became pregnant with our first child, CJ. Something inside of me stirred, and I felt compelled to go to church. The problem I encountered was trying to determine which church to attend, as there were literally hundreds of churches in the community. For example, today the Protestant church has over 33,000 different denominations; which one is true, if any?

Nevertheless, after much reading and research, we ended up in the Anglican (Episcopalian) church, and this is where, ultimately, all four of my children were baptized. Years later, two children were Confirmed in the Roman Catholic Church, as were my wife, daughter, and myself. We left the Anglican Church to become Roman Catholics.

One of my favorite practices in church throughout my time in the Christian church was receiving Communion. Breaking bread with other people is a blessing. Whenever there is an opportunity, I encourage the breaking of bread with others, even if it's breaking sourdough over a bowl of soup, or dipping biscotti in a cup of coffee. Always make time in life to break bread with others. This is a spiritually powerful practice, as it transcends time, place, and culture. There's something above the physical world in the act of breaking bread in community.

I once believed Jesus Christ was God, my salvation, until I visited Israel in 2013. While I was in Jerusalem overlooking the Temple Mount from a distance, I saw man's feeble attempts to reach the heavens by building man-made, theological ladders. What was once the Tower of Babel, I believe today is theology and various "inerrant" scriptures–holy books.

The message, perhaps from God, that resonated in my heart during that moment was, "Be kind." Being kind is simple and complex. It transcends all religions and is perhaps another way of living the Golden Rule: do unto others as you would have them do unto you.

Saint Thomas Aquinas, considered by many to be the greatest Christian theologian to have ever lived, had a spiritual encounter with God and afterward said that everything he had written up until that point was "straw." He never wrote again. Sometimes, God shakes us down to our core and brings us to a more loving, simple faith—such as "be kind." Don't be afraid of a faith/wisdom shift.

Move with the flow of your metaphysical journey.

My experience in Israel began a faith shift. I had a spiritual epiphany and realized that the true gospel is, ultimately, kindness to others, including myself. I cannot say that I am a Christian now, as I have had a faith shift; and truth be told, it was not easy. I no longer spend much time in theology, as I realize it's man-made and divisive to humanity.

I don't regret my time spent in the Christian faith, and certainly the life of Jesus still lives within me. Jesus cared for the poor, the sick, the orphan, the widow, the leper, the sinner, and the immigrant. His message to us was to love God with all our heart, mind, body, and soul, and to love our neighbor as we love ourselves. He said that all else hung on these two commandments. I have prayed many prayers to Jesus and I don't regret them. Many of these prayers were answered. The prayers unanswered were probably answered as well, just not as I would have liked, but perhaps in my best interest. And the truth is, I may yet find my way back to Jesus. I would not discount it.

I believe it is worth the time and effort to read the first five books of the Bible, the Pentateuch, and to read each of the four Gospels: Matthew, Mark, Luke, and John. Much of Western society is founded upon these works, and reading these books will help frame the Western world we live in and perhaps help develop a deeper faith and metaphysical worldview. Recently, I've been drawn to reading the Holy Quran. The Quran's emphasis on mercy and compassion speaks to me in ways I hadn't anticipated. I think the Quran, too, ought to be read and studied.

Today, I consider myself a silent Quaker with Buddhist inclinations and a Catholic mystics soul. I am appreciative of other religious and spiritual traditions. I am a member of a Quaker community, I still periodically attend Mass and Adoration, especially with my mom, I meditate most days, and I willingly sit with Buddhists when I have the opportunity. Hafiz's poetry has been a companion lately. His Sufi wisdom illuminates the divine in everyday moments with playful insight: 'I am a hole in a flute that the Christ's breath moves through.' This resonates with my own journey beyond rigid religious boundaries. My metaphysical foundation has a rich patina, and I am okay with this. I don't feel that I am going to hell. I don't want to be pinned down to a theological identity, and I prefer to live a gospel of kindness to others. Perhaps I am comfortable trusting the love of God with the journey I am on, knowing my path is trending in the right direction. God is oft forgiving and most merciful, no?

Mindfulness meditation, rooted deeply within Buddhism, has been good for me, for my spirit, and it has helped me in many areas of my life. I needed grounding, and Buddhism helped me in this regard. Truth be told, when I needed refuge, a place of comfort when experiencing mild post-traumatic stress following a 25-year fire department career, it was Buddhism that "saved me," not Christianity. Buddha asks his followers to test Buddhism for themselves, content that the proof is in the pudding. Buddhism does not worship a god; it is a philosophy and way of life, a metaphysical foundation.

The Five Precepts of Buddhism that I often repeat to myself are:

Knowing how deeply our lives intertwine, I undertake the following training precept to:

- Protect all life

- Take only what is offered
- Express sexual energy wisely
- Speak truth with kindness
- Not cloud my mind with intoxicants

Buddhism advances the Eightfold Path, leading to clarity and freedom from attachment in life:

- Right understanding
- Right intention
- Right speech
- Right action
- Right livelihood
- Right effort
- Right concentration
- Right mindfulness

Each morning, while taking a shower, I slowly and mindfully repeat a mantra to myself three times: "May I be strong and resilient." I am not intending physical strength, but to be strong in mind, spirit, and character.

Shortly after I retired from the fire department, I became a teacher at a Catholic school. The school is Lasallian in character after Saint Baptiste de La Salle. What was ingrained in me during my short tenure at this school were the Five Core Lasallian Principles. These principles are still part of my foundation today:

- Faith in the presence of God
- Concern for the poor and social justice
- Respect for all persons
- Quality education
- Inclusive community

In sharing the above, it's important that you spend time in your life developing a metaphysical foundation, to know why you believe what you believe. You will come back to this foundation frequently during your lifetime, and it will help you make sense of the world you live in.

Most of America's metaphysical foundation to date has been developed within organized Christianity. Yes, metaphysical foundations may change, faith-wisdom shifts may happen, and if so, it's okay, start anew. One can always keep what has worked for them, drop the rest, and rebuild. If a person were to continue to follow Jesus the rest of their life, they would not be wrong. Jesus is a worthy foundation.

Speaking from experience, if you ever have a faith-wisdom shift in your life, have the courage to go back into your faith and pick out the pieces that are meaningful to you and bring them forward with you. Recreate your faith and wisdom in a manner that works for you and your family.

I want to touch on the "Letter of the Law" vs. the "Spirit of the Law."

In all faith-wisdom traditions, there are liberal and conservative viewpoints. These viewpoints run on a continuum. In every spiritual domain I have dabbled in, I have come across those who are overly concerned with the Letter of the Law. These are the people who would prefer to stone the woman caught in adultery and tell the leper his leprosy is a result of his sin. They bear hard-edged theological swords, and they are ready to cut others down with their knowledge of theology.

Don't be this person.

The Spirit of the Law always precedes the Letter of the Law. The Letter of the Law does not stand without the Spirit of the Law.

For example, Jesus and Buddha are the Spirit of the Law, while the Bible, a book, is the Letter. The Bible points to the Spirit; it is not the Spirit. My grandmother was more "Christian" than most Christians I have met, yet she never beat others down with Biblical sentences, and as far as I know, never read the Bible.

Stated simply: don't be a religious zealot or a dogmatic jackwagon. Be kind in heart and gentle to fellow man. Practice the Spirit of the Law and leave judgment to higher metaphysical powers.

A good basic starting place for a metaphysical foundation is The Golden Rule. The Golden Rule appears to be universal across history and geography. The Golden Rule states that we should do unto others as we would like them to do unto us.

- Brahmanism: "This is the sum of Dharma: Do naught unto others which would cause you pain if done to you."[41]
- Buddhism: "Hurt not others in ways that you yourself would find hurtful."[42]
- Christianity: "So in everything, do to others what you would have them do to you, for this sums up the Law and the Prophets."[43]
- Confucianism: "Do not do to others what you do not want them to do to you."[44]
- Hinduism: "This is the sum of duty: do not do to others what would cause pain if done to you."[45]
- Islam: "None of you truly believes until he loves for his brother what he loves for himself."[46]
- The religion of the Incas: "Do not to another what you would not yourself experience."[47]
- Judaism: "...thou shalt love thy neighbor as thyself."[48]
- Native American Spirituality: "Respect for all life is the foundation."[49]

- Roman Pagan Religion: "The law imprinted on the hearts of all men is to love the members of society as themselves."

A "virtue" is a habit and strong disposition to do good. Virtues guide our conduct and are developed by habitual actions of exercising virtue. The ancient philosophers and the Catholic Church speak of the Four Cardinal Virtues. Cardinal means center, "at the heart of." The Four Cardinal Virtues are at the heart of living a good life. Practice them.

- Prudence: discerning the right and good in each situation and then acting on it.
- Justice: respecting the rights of each person, giving to each person their due.
- Fortitude: strength and resilience in difficult situations, especially when doing right.
- Temperance: balance. Moderating our actions and attraction to pleasure.

In closing, living a good, balanced life necessitates developing a spiritual practice. We are physical and spiritual beings. Developing your spiritual life will provide a metaphysical framework from which you may make sense of the world you live in and answer the most pressing questions that concern humanity.

On your journey, don't forget to pray and offer metta (love) to others.

———

CHAPTER 6
RESILIENCE

SITUATIONAL AWARENESS

In 1991, along with 32 other recruits, I was a new firefighter entering the Phoenix Fire Department's 16-week recruit training program. I loved firefighter training, especially the physicality of it. Mornings were dedicated to workouts and hose lays. Morning runs were done in formation, singing cadence songs. I had just come out of Army basic training and Crash Rescue Fire School, and I knew a few good cadence calls. I'd lead them, loud and proud. It felt good to be young, strong, and courageous. Like a rock, good times.

At the academy, we practiced hose lays over and over again until we could do them in our sleep. We learned the tools and equipment of the trade. We spent hours in the classroom learning about fire behavior and emergency medicine.

What surprised me most—and what I remember most fondly—was our training in the mental aspects of performance (MAP), taught by renowned sports psychologist Gary Mack. Throughout our 16 weeks, Gary would come in a few times a week and teach us how to mentally perform at high levels. He was there because

Phoenix Fire Department's chief, Alan V. Brunacini, was a visionary. Chief "Bruno" believed firefighters were athletes, in every sense of the word. He wanted to provide recruits with all the tools they'd need not just to do the job, but to sustain themselves, physically, mentally, and emotionally for a lifetime of public service.

Several of Gary's lessons focused on breath work. Imagine being taught how to breathe and realizing you were never taught to breathe well. He'd say, "Breathe and focus." It became a pillar of our training. Years later, on the fireground, I'd step off the truck at a complex emergency incident and say to myself: "Breathe and focus." And that's what I'd do.

THE WORK

Part 1: Foundations of Resilience

Being in, on, near, or around water

pools, rivers, lakes, oceans

is healing to the mind, body, and soul.[1]

Resilient outcome =

work well

play well

love well

expect well.

. . .

Fall down seven times

get up eight

Rise eight

Rise 8.[2]

Be happy and healthy

live in the present

build resilience

for an increasingly complex world.

"Resilience is the capacity of a dynamic system

to adapt successfully

to disturbances that threaten function

viability

or development.

The biggest surprise in resilience research:

how ordinary it is.

This is good news."[3]

"In the presence of significant adversity

resilience is the capacity of individuals

to navigate their way to resources

that sustain well-being

and negotiate for those resources

to be provided in culturally meaningful ways."[4]

Resilience comes from resilire

Latin: To rebound

to bounce back.

In engineering

materials are resilient

when they resist breaking

under stress

and return to original form.

In ecology

resilience is the capacity

of a system

to absorb disturbance

reorganize

and persist in a similar state.

Resilience is:

Persistence

Resistance

Recovery

Adaptation

Transformation[5]

Adversity + doing well after adversity = resilience.

If there is no adversity

there can be no resilience

if adversity has been experienced

but the person (system) is not doing well

resilience is not yet.

Recovery, adaptation, and transformation

after system disturbance

is resilience.

Resilience is a (multi-systems) process.

Bring to mind someone

who has experienced adversity

and today

they are doing well.

What was their adversity?

How are they doing well?

What helped them recover?

Through these narratives

we build resilience vicariously.

There are judgments made in resilience:

Who decides what counts as adversity?

Who defines "doing well"?

Is resilience internal, external

or both?

How long does resilience take?

Who decides

how long it takes?

These questions matter.

Resilience mythology:

Individual grit and tenacity

alone

are enough.

Resilience reality:

It's about relationships

resources

reserves

rest

recovery

and ruggedness.

Resilience is

about support

about others

connections

community

standing shoulder to shoulder

with others.

We are misled by myths of heroic resilience

in reality

resilience comes from the everyday

the ordinary:

Relationships

resources

and support.

. . .

Most people do well after trauma

but they may be left with scars or shadows.

Sometimes at noon

the shadow is not there

it's not seen.

Sometimes at 3 pm

the shadow is long.

Such is living

after trauma

after adversity

after adversities

plural.

Resilience focuses on what is going right

on the strengths of a person.

Resilience is growing edges.

Take what is working

and grow edges

from there.

The brain can be rewired

neuroplasticity:

Stretchy brain.

Part 2: Stress, Perception, and Adaptation

Stress is not what happens to us,

it's how we interpret what happens to us.

An event + our perception of the event = stress.

Events are neutral.

It's our thoughts that create meaning.

Thoughts create feelings,

Feelings drive behavior.

In the space between what happens

and how we respond

we have power.

Change is constant.

Even joy can cause stress.

Not all stress is bad.

Eustress enhances performance.

Distress degrades it.

Two kinds of stressors:

Acute and chronic.

Exposure to the right kind

of stress

at the right dose

in a crawl, walk, run approach

builds strength.

Stress inoculation, Steeling.

The right amount of stress

develops resilience for the future.

We need some stress

to learn and grow.

Stressful experience + effective recovery =

enhanced resilience

Resilience is reduced by incomplete recovery.

You must recover.

Train the stress response:

Crawl

Walk

Run.

Why don't zebras get ulcers?

Because zebras respond to real lions,

not thoughts of lions.[6]

Social media?

Digital lions,

Not real.

Arousal Control Sequence:

Check in

Ground

Breathe.

Check in:

How are you?

What's going on inside your body?

Where do your feelings show up in your body?

. . .

Ground:

Stable position

Relaxed but ready.

Feel the earth.

Let your brainstem know

it's okay.

Breathe

in through the nose

slowly

deeply

and completely

hold it briefly

let it out the nose

slowly

deeply

and completely.

Thoughts become emotions.

Emotions become physiology,

they show up in the body.

Physiology becomes performance.

. . .

Keep doing the little things.

1% adds up.

You don't need a breakthrough,

You need a process.

Apply strategy.

Addressing stress:

Change yourself;

Make the best use of resources;

Change your world to create more resources;

And when all else fails,

change what you want.[7]

Part 3: The Mental and Emotional Toolkit

Mental health days are real

Take them.

Adopt a growth mindset

Be willing to learn and grow.

. . .

Meditate

Practice breath work

Visualize doing well.

Write haiku

Keep a gratitude journal

Write, journal, blog.

Develop calming self-talk

Positive visualization

Repetition

Ritual.

Chin up

Shoulders back

Smile

Stand tall.

Set a few small goals

Conduct after-action reviews

Debrief

Talk it out.

You become what you consistently think about.

Anxiety is related to thoughts.
In modern life, we suffer from
chronic, perceived, emotional stress.
Social media amplifies this.

Your mind, body, and soul will heal
if you give yourself time and space to do so.

Mindfulness meditation
regular, ongoing practice
can be very healing.

The issues are in the tissues
The body keeps the score[8]
What fires together wires together.[9]

Images and sounds reduce stress
A bird on a flagpole

wind in the flag

a river running

These sights and sounds

soothe.

Be patient with yourself

Love yourself

Be kind to yourself.

Have good, positive narratives

playing in your mind.

If you're not meditating

doing yoga

or practicing breath work regularly

you're behind the curve.

Part 4: Body as Foundation

Exercise 3 to 4 times per week, at least.

Play sports

Be less sedentary

Walk

Hike

Swim.

Get in the water, water is healing.

Sauna

Jacuzzi

Pool.

Get a therapeutic massage.

Train with purpose,

Train with intensity.

Intensity makes a difference

Do targeted work with intensity.

Pace, don't race.

Slow and steady wins the race.

Rome wasn't built in a day.

Inch by inch

it's a cinch.

Yard by yard

it's hard.

Tortoise

and the hare.

Why do we train?

To prepare the human

to move efficiently

effectively

and safely

through the environment.

Quality

Quantity

Timing.

Warm up

Work hard

Cool down.

There are no secrets here.

We need consistency for longevity.

Train purposefully.

Your desk at work does not own you.
Ghost your desk
Don't let your desk
dictate how you move.

Age-related decline exists
but it doesn't have to be inevitable.
Challenge it every day.

We can prepare our bodies
to be more efficient
and resilient.

Pain = protection.
Listen to your body when it hurts.

One hour per week of resistance training
reduces cardiovascular risk.

Eat well

work that body

thrive in the mind.

Set goals

for work

for life.

Set goals

Build routines

Debrief.

Get 1% better every day.

Use it or lose it.

You must practice.

Part 5: Sleep and Recovery

Sleep is important,

Very important.

Rest is not optional

It's when repair happens.

Micro-breakdown occurs during sleep

That's where healing lives.

Sleep architecture:

The brain runs on a 24-hour cycle.

Light entrains the system.

Light is the single most important

external cue for healthy sleep.

Melatonin peaks in the middle of the night.

Screens (phones) suppress melatonin

Blue light delays it.

Eyes are receptors

They tell the brain:

Stay awake.

Or:

It's time to sleep.

Controlling light = controlling sleep.

. . .

Expose your eyes to natural light during the day.

Avoid screens at night

No phones in bed

No televisions in the room.

Sleep should be:

Uninterrupted

Regular

Same bedtime

Same wake time.

Light at night is a carcinogen.

Tactical napping:

Short naps (<30 min)

or full cycles (90 min).

Pre-sleep routine:

- Turn lights down

- Make a list

- Plan the next day

- Shower, brush teeth

- Read

- Avoid screens

- Go to bed without your phone

Associate your bed only with sleep.

No TV

no phones

no scrolling

No social media

no bringing out the thought

lions

before bed.

If you take melatonin,

take only when you have six hours to sleep,

at night.[10]

Instead of macro moves

make micro adjustments.

We need rhythms and routines in life.

. . .

Sleep is so important.

So deeply important.

Alcohol impairs sleep.

Hydrate or die-drate.

Stay hydrated.

Part 6: Food as Medicine

Good food is essential to good health.

Period.

Eat healthy

Eat more fiber

Eat more fruits and vegetables

Limit junk food.

Easier said than done

but still true.

Eat less

Move more.

. . .

Deep nutrition.

Know what it is

know how to cook for yourself.

When you need healing

your body needs deep nutrition.

Hint: Good homemade soup

long-cooked with bones.

Cooking healthy food

especially soup

is healing.

Saturated fats are not the enemy.

They're good for you:

Olive oil

Avocado

Seeds

Fish

Peanut butter.

Olive oil is very good for you.

Don't cook with vegetable oil

It's not good for you.

Whole grains are high in fiber

Fiber supports healthy aging.

Low vitamin D levels

increase the risk of depression and mood swings.

Stopping at the pub?

Practice "two and out."

Two beers then head home.

Alcohol impairs:

- Sleep

- Recovery

- Hydration

- Decision-making

- Hunger regulation

. . .

Drink in moderation

Don't smoke or vape

Don't do drugs.

Don't get big and bulky strong

Get lean and fit.

Work out

eat

rest

recover

repeat.

Part 7: Social Resilience and Community

Resilience:

Better outcomes happen

when we're surrounded by

family and friends.

Why?

Because we share

We talk

We process

We're not alone.

Resilience is about relationships.

Always has been

Always will be.

Protective factors in our life

buffer risk.

They lead to resilience

They include people

They include place.

Risk factors increase

illness, injury, harm.

Risk begets risk

But protective factors beget strength.

Asset building is strategy.

Build relationships

Build resources

Minimize risk.

There are two kinds of protective factors:
Rugged factors and Resources.[11]

Rugged factors:

A powerful identity

Altruism

Communication skills

Conscientiousness

Cooperation

Creativity

Critical thinking

Decision-making

Empathy

Flexibility

Goal-setting

Gratitude

Humor

Spirituality

Self-regulation

Morality

Perseverance

Hope

Optimism

Physical activity

Positive emotions

Problem-solving

Self-actualization

Self-care

Self-efficacy

Confidence

Resources:

Community

Peer support

Access to healthcare

Outdoor spaces

Accountability

Advocacy

Limited social media

Family

Elders

Culture

Education

Opportunity

Good-enough parenting

Housing

Jobs

Mentors

Making decisions

Using talents

Routines

Physical safety

Nutrition

Respect

Expectations

Relationships

Citizenship

When problems are few,

Ruggedness is enough.

When problems are many

Resources are necessary.

Of the the two

Resources are best.

Serve others

Volunteer

Walk a shelter dog.

Spend time with family and friends

Spend time with pets

Spend time in nature.

Go to church

Or other spiritual gathering

Connect with your faith-wisdom community.

Talk to a mentor

A coach

A counselor.

Seek peer support

from people you trust.

Debrief

Talk it out

Share your story.

Resilience lives in connection.

Part 8: Resilient Moves – The Practice

Take a mental health day

Take a walk

Take a breath.

Adopt a growth mindset

Read a book

Take a class

Learn a new language

Learn something new.

Walk

Hike

Swim

Slow walks.

Get in the water

water is healing.

Volunteer

Serve others

Walk a shelter dog

Help someone

Help yourself by helping.

Spend time:

with pets

with people

with family

with friends

with mentors.

Talk it out

Share your story

Debrief

Speak with someone you trust.

Get good sleep

Take breaks

Rest

Recover.

Write

Journal

Blog

Write haiku poems

Write your way back to yourself.

Practice breathing

Practice visualizing

Practice gratitude

Practice.

Pray

Meditate

Reflect.

Develop calming self-talk

Positive visualization.

Laugh

Listen to music.

Set a few small goals
Set a routine
Establish rhythms.

Do the little things
1% better every day
It adds up.

Eat healthy:
reds, blues, and greens
Cook
Bake
Garden.

Go shopping
Yes, shopping can be restorative.

Socialize, lightly.

Go to the doctor

Check in with your body

Check in with your mind.

Apply strategy to life

Live on purpose

Move on purpose.

Be kind to yourself

Love yourself

Be patient

You're doing better than you think.

Keep kicking and scratching

Endure

Persevere

Grit

Sisu[12]

Be tenacious.

Keep moving

Keep breathing

Keep going.

. . .

Closing Meditation

Resilience is not rare

It is not heroic

It is human.

It is the sum of small acts

done with purpose.

Karma!

Fall down seven times

Get up eight

Rise eight

Rise 8.

TAILBOARD: GRIT

The language and meaning of "resilience" has proven to be some-what nebulous and amorphous, a challenging word to define and gain consensus on. In fact, I was recently listening to a conversation where a marketing company admitted, "Resilience is tough to brand." Further, one could make the argument "resilience" has become a fetish and co-opted by the neoliberal establishment.

Why do unjust systems necessitate the resilience of some dispro-portionately?

This got me thinking about the word grit. Would grit be more accessible in everyday conversation? Easier to understand? Is grit a better word to use when talking about resilience?

So I did what any reflective, modern philosopher does, I asked my Facebook friends. I posted a simple comparison between "resilience" and "grit," and invited people to share what each word meant to them.

Valid study? No. But not nothing either. Call it qualitative research from the cheap seats.

Here's what my friends had to say about grit:

- Courage
- Determination
- Strength
- Bravery
- Persistence
- Guts
- Resilience
- Stamina
- Holding true to the end
- Perseverance
- Setting a goal and doing whatever it takes
- Tough
- Honesty

Also in the mix were: sandpaper, dirt, "weird food," something that needs cleaning, Alabama breakfast, and "a workout at my gym."

Now here's what they said about resilience:

- Withstand almost anything
- Crisis management

- Keep going
- Strong; can handle difficulty
- Bounce back
- Mindset to start over or try a new way
- Look forward, not back
- Not just withstanding challenges, but growing from them
- Adaptation
- Resistance
- Bend but don't break
- Make lemonade out of lemons

I'd say my friends have a pretty good intuitive grasp on both concepts. But the distinction is important.

Resilience, as we understand it through research and practice, is deeply connected to context, to the environments we live and move within, and to the support systems around us. It's about how we access, navigate, and negotiate for resources that help us during life's most difficult moments.

Resilience is not an individual trait. It's a combination of protective factors, buffers, and moderators in our lives—families, communities, systems. Resilience is about resources, relationships (support), rest, and recovery.

Grit, on the other hand, tends to reflect something more personal. More internal. More individual. It's the result of a powerful mindset, something that originates inside and expresses itself through effort and perseverance.

Both resilience and grit are important. We need support and resources to help us in times of need, and we also need an internal mindset that is tenacious.

Dr. Angela Duckworth, who has studied grit exhaustively, suggests grit may predict success more reliably than IQ or raw talent.[13] Resilience researchers might argue with this suggestion, but her point stands: grit matters.

It brings to mind an old wrestling quote I've always liked, "Hard work beats talent when talent doesn't work hard."

My favorite definition of grit comes from my fifth-grade teacher, someone I still correspond with. She lives in a log cabin in the Rocky Mountains and knows a thing or two about grit. She once told me: "There's an edge of defiance and fierceness in grit... like unbridled determination and perseverance in the face of adversity."

In her TED talk, The Key to Success? Grit,[14] Angela Duckworth defines grit this way:

- Grit is passion and perseverance for long-term goals.
- Grit is stamina.
- Grit is sticking with your future—day in and day out—not just for a week, but for years.
- Grit is living life like it's a marathon, not a sprint.

Interestingly, in her talk she admits she doesn't know how to teach it.

But that's our jumping-off point.

Grit is not about talent. It's not about intellect. It's about mindset. It's about how we respond to adversity. And most importantly, it's about how we internalize failure.

I'm a retired firefighter. Over my career, I responded to more than 15,000 emergency incidents.

I worked with some very gritty firefighters.

When a community experiences an emergency, they call the fire department with the expectation that the problem will be solved. That's the community mindset. And firefighters? We share it. We show up believing this emergency will be mitigated. There is no quit, only grit.

That mindset is cultivated through training and repetition. Through mentorship. Through thousands of moments of both success and failure, on the street, and in the real world.

When I served as Training Chief, we designed scenarios that deliberately placed firefighters in situations where their tactics would "fail." Not to demoralize them, but to build the mental muscle required to adapt, to pivot, to keep going. They learned to shift strategy. They learned that the problem can be solved, even if the original plan doesn't work.

Failure wasn't failure. It was an inflection point, a hinge, a redirect, an opportunity to move in a new direction toward problem mitigation. What firefighters learned was that they could adjust to "failures" accordingly, and as a result, failures were not actually failures, they were opportunities.

The mindset we built was this: We're going to solve the problem. If what we're doing isn't working, we don't quit, we adjust.

In that way, grit becomes a visible manifestation of an internal mindset. It's a refusal to let a "no" be the final answer. And that lesson holds across every domain of life.

Take Chris Byron, a Canadian educator who works with middle school students in outdoor, nature-based settings. He intentionally builds physical challenges that allow students to fail—on purpose.

Why? Because he wants them to practice failure. To learn how to respond to it. Because life guarantees failure. Chris says, "Physical challenges foster grit. And grit is better than talent." I like that.[15]

Success in life is likely a determinate of grit—that unbridled determination and perseverance in the face of adversity. Grit is the visible manifestation of an internal mindset. Internal mindsets come about through training and repetition, especially as it relates to what is perceived as "failure." Gritty cultures can foster gritty individuals.

There is no failure, only acceptance that our strategy or tactics might need to change.

We need a gritty mindset, and loads of resources and support in life.

———

CHAPTER 7
MINIMALISM

SITUATIONAL AWARENESS

Several months back, on a Friday night, my wife and I visited the local chophouse for happy hour. On this particular evening, the chophouse was running a special on a local craft beer. The beer was Migration Patterns, brewed by Crane Brewing in Raytown, Missouri.

Migration Patterns is a very hoppy IPA, the kind of beer that bites back. I love beer like this. In fact, Migration Patterns is easily one of my favorite IPAs.

This brief encounter with this very good craft beer led me to philosophically ponder crane migration patterns, like the real birds, which I knew nothing about. Of course, being the geek that I am, I read up on cranes and their migration patterns because, well, this is just how I am wired.

Turns out, sandhill cranes are actually quite fascinating. They migrate twice a year, with some flying 5,000 miles from Siberia to Mexico. These cranes average 200-300 miles per day, and with a good tailwind, they can cover 500 miles. The journey is dangerous for the cranes, mainly due to weather and hunters. Impressively, sandhill cranes can live 20-40 years.

Consider this: sandhill cranes live 20-40 years and fly 5,000 miles twice per year. And do you know what they take for their journey? Their material possessions?

Nothing.

Compare and contrast. We, humans, are on this earth for 74-78 years on average. We don't migrate twice per year; and as a general rule, we stay in only a few places over a lifetime. Despite this, we have many possessions. Many, many things.[1]

THE WORK

Practice voluntary poverty

minimalism

and simplicity.

Read three books:

Journeys of Simplicity[2]

The Abundance of Less[3]

Less is More[4]

Use it up

Wear it out

Make it do

Or do without.[5]

The sandhill crane flies
5,000 miles twice a year
and carries nothing.[6]

Embrace less.
Less is more.[7]
More
feel good in the soul
smile on the face
and beauty in life.
Yes, less is more.

"The things you own,
end up owning you."[8]

Simplify
Simplify
Simplify.[9]

TAILBOARD: BALANCED MINIMALISM AND MINIMAL TRAVEL

Balanced Minimalism

I've been reading and reflecting more on minimalism lately. The definitions vary, but at its heart, minimalism is about divesting yourself of those things, including relationships, that don't bring freedom or joy. It's about creating space for what matters most.

And I like it. I really do.

But I've also noticed something: like anything else, minimalism can become an extreme. I've seen photos of minimalist homes where the only piece of furniture was a single chair. No pictures, no books, no blankets, no color. Just a chair. That's not simplicity, that's sterility. It reminds me that minimalism, if we're not careful, can become as obsessive as hoarding. Hoarders fill every inch of their homes with things. Extremist minimalists strip it all away. Both can miss the point.

What separates the two? Minimalism gets a cultural head nod. It's cool to be minimalist. Hoarding… not so much.

But let me get philosophical for a second.

Before modernity, philosophers and theologians assumed an objective reality existed outside themselves. There really were things in the world, things with their own truth, beauty, and purpose. But along came Descartes with "I think, therefore I am," and suddenly truth became internal, subjective. We started building worlds inside our heads and treating everything outside as optional, even questioning if things existed.

Here's the reality: there are things that exist in this world whether we believe in them or not. We can have intelligent conversations about real things because they're actually there. For example, my wife and I continue to talk about the beautiful furniture and hardwood floors at our favorite coffee shop in Montana. Not because the furniture and floors are in our heads, but because they are real!

So what's the point?

The point is, it's okay to surround ourselves with things that are beautiful, useful, spiritual, or sentimental. Things can speak to us. A favorite mug, a photograph, a carved cross. These things have stories. They point us to the Divine, to memory, to meaning. They're not clutter, they're anchors in our lives.

That's what I mean by balanced minimalism.

Balanced minimalism means carefully considering the things and relationships in my life and only divesting myself of what doesn't bring me closer to Sacred Depth, Creative Mystery, my family, or my friends. Closer to what is true, good, and beautiful. It's a new framework I'm experimenting with, and honestly, I'm enjoying it. I've started slowly working through the house, filling bins with things that no longer serve.

Here's the checklist I use:

1. Is it beautiful?
2. Is it useful? Have I used it in the last two years?
3. Does it help me feel spiritual or point me to God?
4. Is it irreplaceably sentimental?
5. Do I have too many of them? Can I keep one instead of three?

That's the internal audit.

Another practice I've adopted is buying quality. For example, I could buy three long-sleeved shirts from Kohl's for fifty bucks with a coupon. Or—I could buy one organic cotton Patagonia shirt that fits right, feels good, and lasts longer than all three combined. It takes up less space, feels better to wear, and holds value over time.

Travel has helped shape this mindset, too. In many parts of the world, people wear one outfit for three days. In America, we think we need a new outfit every day—sometimes two. But simplicity is normal elsewhere. It's efficient. It's even elegant.

Minimalism and voluntary simplicity are "long-view" practices. They don't happen overnight, but they do happen—with intention.

Virtue, as Aquinas reminds us, is the mean between excess and deficiency. Minimalism isn't about asceticism for its own sake. It's about finding balance.

"Use it up. Wear it out. Make it do. Or do without." "Simplify. Simplify. Simplify."

Minimal Travel

Morning, boys.

I was just telling Mom—look how cute we are in our little Montana house, sitting at the kitchen table with coffee and computers. The sun's up, trees are deep green, birds are singing, dogs sprawled across the floor. Your sister's quietly doodling in her room.

It's Labor Day—hail to the workers—and a good day to be still. But you ever notice how sometimes short weeks feel longer than full ones? I don't know why that is. Just one of life's mysteries.

Anyway, you guys are on my mind today. Maybe it's the season. Maybe it's the pace of life lately. But I've been thinking about travel, and more specifically, how we travel.

From Halifax to Stockholm, Geneva to Kyiv, San Francisco to Jerusalem—I've learned that to travel well, you have to travel light. There's a certain freedom in packing intentionally. It makes the movement smoother, the mindset clearer. You start to realize: the less you carry, the freer you feel.

That's not just true for backpacks. It's true for life.

When our house sells—and Montana becomes the new home base, I want you to come visit often. Stay as long as you like. This is a four-bedroom house and we only use two. The other two? Yours. We'll cook for you, spoil you, take you into the mountains. We'll hunt, fish, hike, ski Red Lodge and Big Sky. You name it. Alberta's just a day's drive north. Yellowstone, Glacier, Grand Tetons—right out the back door.

So I've been thinking. When the house sells, I'd like to get each of you a quality travel backpack. Something you'll use for years, across continents. I'm looking at the Osprey Farpoint 40L. It's the most reputable minimalist travel pack out there. Forty liters is plenty of space to travel for weeks at a time. Check it out and let me know your thoughts. Or if you find a different one that fits better, I'm all ears.

If you're going minimalist, you've gotta think through every item. That includes underwear. Yep. I'm getting each of you two pairs of ExOfficio Men's Travel Underwear. Rumor has it, you could travel the world for a year with just two pairs. (I wouldn't test it, but that's the rumor.)

Add some good wool socks—Smartwool—and a solid pair of travel shoes, and you're good to go.

There's a blog I like by a guy who traveled the world with nothing more than a 20-liter pack. It's called 20 Liter Life.[10] Worth checking out.

Here's the deeper point of this Dad-rant: I want you thinking now about traveling lightly, not just for the sake of mobility, but for the kind of freedom it gives you.

We're not built to be owned by our stuff.

"The things you own, end up owning you." Less is more. It's more smile on the face. More beauty in life. More soul.

So yeah, start thinking about your travel gear. Let me know if the Osprey looks good to you. Pick your color. Or find your own.

But more than anything, keep your life light enough that you can always pack up and go.

Love you guys, Dad

———

CHAPTER 8
POETRY

SITUATIONAL AWARENESS

I have visions.

I was driving to Red Lodge, MT early one Saturday morning to attend Search and Rescue training with the Red Lodge Fire Dept. It was winter, snow on the ground, cold. As I came into town, driving slowly, I passed an old man with a big gray beard in a Jeep Grand Wagoneer, the kind with wood panels. Sitting next to him in the front seat was an old yellow Labrador retriever, gray in the muzzle. In that moment, I thought to myself: this is what I aspire to. I want to be an old man driving with my dog in the mountains while my wife is at home playing with the grandkids and my kids are up on the mountain skiing.

I have visions. Here's what I see:

Our home is a warm and comfortable home. It's charming. It has character. The house sits on a little bit of land. There is a library, a special room where I sit quietly and read. The flooring is hardwood. There is, of course, a fireplace. This is a place that really feels like home. It's where Victoria and I will live out the rest of our days, where the kids will come home to visit.

The visions keep coming.

I love my wife, of course, and she still teaches down the road. I teach 4th grade and religion and philosophy part-time at the local college one evening a week. I still blog and write books. I work with my hands and my faith is contemplative.

I live to be 88 years old, and then, surrounded by my very large family and friends, I begin my crane migration. I fall asleep and immediately I am hugging my son, Coop. After days of hugging, I meet God face to face. He hugs me and tells me, "Well done."

I have tears streaming down my face. So does God.

THE WORK

Lifeboats

Is it okay that I cry tears of sorrow and despair?

That I raise my fists and shake my hands and curse God,

for being so absent, amongst the pain in this world?

A lifeboat sits, brimming with human flesh,

refugees, fleeing violence, in the Mediterranean,

whilst policy makers decide—whom to accept.

A child, with large brown eyes, innocent,

she does not know You; should she?

Will she die today?

. . .

America. Long the land of the free and the home of the brave.

The land of the free, and the home of the brave.

America.

Brave? Christian souls, saved, personal relationships with Jesus,

parked in mega-church parking lots, pastors selling books,

rock band music blaring, on a Sunday,

parking lot littered with Mercedes Benz,

hands raised in worship and praise.

While lifeboats, brimming with refugees,

float on the coast of Italy

waiting, bobbing, up and down, up and down,

whilst the policy makers politic.

America, the home of the brave.

The brave, barely able to vote,

escaping bullets during high school biology,

whilst the cowards Tweet and politic.

The hyenas, the cackling base, dark souls,

ears bent toward the copper coat,

whilst the children run, toward the lifeboats,

bobbing, up and down, and escaping bullets,

in America.

The soothsayers and the oracles,

the mystics, the shamans,

they hurt, they cry tears of sorrow,

because they know.

They know, that whilst the children

bob and run from the bullets,

the policy makers politic

and the cowards Tweet.

God weeps over the earth, brimming with flesh,

bobbing and weaving, waiting on the coast,

for the policy makers to politic,

and the cowards to Tweet.

Will we live today?

Great Grace

Good morning, Great Grace.

As I walk this morning, I am grateful and thankful
to feel my body move through space and time.
It feels good for me to walk.

I am feeling the sun shine warm upon my face,
touching my wrinkles and brown spots with kindness.

The birds are singing, each his own tune,
but together a great symphony.

Dear Lizard, warming yourself on the pavement,
I see you and I like you. You make me smile.

Quail families are scurrying about,
7, 8, 9, 10 little chickens following mom.

I hear a child, screaming in playful delight.
I hear her say, "Daaaaaaaaaaaaaad."

I think of my own family and children,

that I have a wife to love me and balance me,

and children who love me and tell me so.

My puppies, my sweet puppies,

oh how I love your loyal souls.

That I can write, and put my thoughts on paper,

I am thankful.

Whatever all of this is,

it is what I worship,

what I call Great Grace.

I don't understand the theology of Great Grace,

only presence.

You, Great Grace, have not abandoned me.

You stay with me always,

though sometimes easier to breathe in than others.

Your dark night is filled with stars

and cool wind that tickles my skin;

and this simple gift is appreciated.

. . .

I don't know the theology of what happens when I die,

or even why I am here,

but I pray that you will take me, Great Grace,

and carry me on your currents when it is my time.

This, I set my heart upon.

Soul of a Family

Emanating effortless peace and grace,

moving in rhythm,

beautiful.

The only way to live a family life of grace and peace,

is to live in a state of grace and peace.

A healthy family sacrifices for one another,

loves each other unconditionally, and forgives often.

The ability to sacrifice, love unconditionally, and truly forgive

is only possible when we understand

that the same has been done for us.

. . .

True beauty and the soul of a healthy family

flows from true beauty and the soul of the Divine.

I have no other words with which to say it.

Surfing the Wave

Some people dream of surfing that wave

standing on liquid fearless and brave.

We'll see glittering sun in the water's reflection

reminding us all that we're made in perfection.

Catching the curl is the greatest reward

with toes on the nose of a slippery board.[1]

Irish Blessing

May the road rise up to meet you,

may the wind be always at your back,

may the sun shine warm upon your face,

the rains fall soft upon your fields,

and until we meet again,

may God hold you in the palm of His hand.[2]

. . .

For Whom the Bell Tolls

No man is an island,

Entire of itself.

Each is a piece of the continent,

A part of the main.

If a clod be washed away by the sea,

Europe is the less,

As well as if a promontory were,

As well as if a manor of thine own

Or of thine friend's were.

Each man's death diminishes me,

For I am involved in mankind.

Therefore, send not to know

For whom the bell tolls,

It tolls for thee.[3]

The Man in the Arena

It is not the critic who counts;

not the man who points out how the strong man stumbles,

or where the doer of deeds could have done them better.

. . .

The credit belongs to the man who is actually in the arena,

whose face is marred by dust and sweat and blood;

who strives valiantly; who errs,

who comes short again and again,

because there is no effort without error and shortcoming;

but who does actually strive to do the deeds;

who knows great enthusiasms, the great devotions;

who spends himself in a worthy cause;

who at the best knows in the end the triumph of high achievement,

and who at the worst, if he fails, at least fails while daring greatly,

so that his place shall never be with those cold and timid souls

who neither know victory nor defeat.[4]

The Puppy Asleep

The puppy asleep

pushing his feet against

the willow tree.[5]

In the Winter River

In the winter river

pulled up and thrown away—

a red turnip.[6]

My Bones

My bones

feel the quilts—

a frosty night.[7]

The Road Not Taken

Two roads diverged in a yellow wood,

And sorry I could not travel both

And be one traveler, long I stood

And looked down one as far as I could

To where it bent in the undergrowth;

Then took the other, as just as fair,

And having perhaps the better claim,

Because it was grassy and wanted wear;

Though as for that the passing there

Had worn them really about the same,

.   .   .

And both that morning equally lay

In leaves no step had trodden black.

Oh, I kept the first for another day!

Yet knowing how way leads on to way,

I doubted if I should ever come back.

I shall be telling this with a sigh

Somewhere ages and ages hence:

Two roads diverged in a wood, and I—

I took the one less traveled by,

And that has made all the difference.[8]

If—

If you can keep your head when all about you

Are losing theirs and blaming it on you,

If you can trust yourself when all men doubt you,

But make allowance for their doubting too;

If you can wait and not be tired by waiting,

Or being lied about, don't deal in lies,

Or being hated, don't give way to hating,

And yet don't look too good, nor talk too wise:

.   .   .

If you can dream—and not make dreams your master;

If you can think—and not make thoughts your aim;

If you can meet with Triumph and Disaster

And treat those two impostors just the same;

If you can bear to hear the truth you've spoken

Twisted by knaves to make a trap for fools,

Or watch the things you gave your life to, broken,

And stoop and build 'em up with worn-out tools:

If you can make one heap of all your winnings

And risk it on one turn of pitch-and-toss,

And lose, and start again at your beginnings

And never breathe a word about your loss;

If you can force your heart and nerve and sinew

To serve your turn long after they are gone,

And so hold on when there is nothing in you

Except the Will which says to them: 'Hold on!'

If you can talk with crowds and keep your virtue,

Or walk with Kings—nor lose the common touch,

If neither foes nor loving friends can hurt you,

If all men count with you, but none too much;

If you can fill the unforgiving minute

With sixty seconds' worth of distance run,

Yours is the Earth and everything that's in it,

And—which is more—you'll be a Man, my son!⁹

Invictus

Out of the night that covers me,

Black as the pit from pole to pole,

I thank whatever gods may be

For my unconquerable soul.

In the fell clutch of circumstance

I have not winced nor cried aloud.

Under the bludgeonings of chance

My head is bloody, but unbowed.

Beyond this place of wrath and tears

Looms but the Horror of the shade,

And yet the menace of the years

Finds and shall find me unafraid.

It matters not how strait the gate,

How charged with punishments the scroll,

I am the master of my fate,

I am the captain of my soul.[10]

The Tiger and the Strawberry

A man was walking across a field when he encountered a tiger.

He fled, with the tiger in pursuit.

Coming to a precipice, he caught hold of the root of a wild vine

and swung himself over the edge.

The tiger sniffed at him from above.

Trembling, the man looked down to where,

far below, another tiger was waiting to eat him.

Only the vine sustained him.

Two mice, one white and one black,

began to gnaw away at the vine.

The man saw a luscious strawberry near him.

Holding the vine with one hand,

he plucked the strawberry with the other and ate it.

How sweet it tasted![11]

The Invitation (Excerpt) by Oriah Mountain Dreamer

It doesn't interest me to know where you live or how much money you have.

I want to know if you can get up after the night of grief and despair,

weary and bruised to the bone,

and do what needs to be done to feed the children.

It doesn't interest me who you know or how you came to be here.

I want to know if you will stand in the centre of the fire with me

and not shrink back.[12]

TAILBOARD: THE INVITATION BY ORIAH MOUNTAIN DREAMER

Firefighters call fire "the dragon." It's a beast we fight, we slay. For example, a firefighter could be coming into work to begin their shift and the off-going fire crew says, "We slayed the dragon last night." What they mean is, they had a fire they fought.

When fighting fire, there are generally two strategies. Offensive firefighting is going into the building with hose lines to find the fire and put water on it, and hopefully, put the fire out. Defensive firefighting is recognizing that the fire is too advanced to safely enter the building, and the fire is fought from the outside at safe positions.

When fighting fire "offensively," it can become quite demanding when a firefighter actually finds the fire. The fire can be extremely hot, and advancing to the seat of the fire, firefighters must have the courage to "stand in the center of the fire and not shrink back."

The reason I like this poem so much by Oriah is that it speaks to me as a firefighter—I understand it.

I can remember being at work, the fire station, running calls all night long and just getting crushed. I would come home weary and bruised to the bone, but that was my work—that's what I had to do to feed my children and put a roof over their heads. But that's the point—I had a "why." I had dreams and goals for my family. A person can withstand a terrible beating in life if they have a 'why.'

During this time of crazy politics, charged political discourse, and animosity toward fellow man, I encourage you to either know or find your "why." Hope and dream and live. I love the occasional and well-placed f- you! I think the greatest "f- you" you could give to The System, The Matrix, and The Man right now would be to have hope, and to dare to chase after YOUR dreams. Be autonomous. Think for yourself. Live, love, and learn. Be free.

My son, Carse, once cast a vision that sounded crazy at the time. He said he wanted to own a small cottage on Coronado Island, have a daughter, and an Alaskan Malamute named Apollo. I chuckled that he "saw" an Alaskan Malamute in San Diego. But hey, he did more than most, he cast a vision. He dared to dream.

It's a start, and this is where a 1,000-mile journey begins, with the first step. Dare to start.

At any rate, rather than despair about life, which is where so many people are at today, have hope and live your life. Chase your dreams and stay true to yourself.

Yesterday was a tough day for me. It was just one of those really suck days. "Mama told me there would be days like this..."

The Invitation by Oriah Mountain Dreamer reminds me that in life there will be days—perhaps months, maybe even years—where we have to stand in the center of the fire and not shrink back. We have to get up, over and over again, weary and bruised to the bone, and live a life of hope and meaning.

———

CHAPTER 9
SCREENS & TECHNOLOGY

SITUATIONAL AWARENESS

As a father, and a teacher, I like to introduce my kids to good thinking and good thinkers. I want them to learn from others, understand the world, and be able to think creatively, deeply, and clearly in the face of complexity.

On March 24, 2016, I took my youngest son, Coop—16 at the time—to the Loft Cinema in Tucson, Arizona, for a sold-out screening of Citizenfour,[1] the Oscar-winning documentary about Edward Snowden and the NSA surveillance leaks. What made it especially powerful was that Glenn Greenwald, Pulitzer Prize-winning journalist and one of the film's central figures, was there in person. After the film, he took the stage for a live discussion and answered audience questions. Coop got to sit in the room and listen to Greenwald talk about government surveillance and the right to privacy.

The very next night, I brought my son Carse, then 18, to another event, this one hosted by the University of Arizona's College of Social and Behavioral Sciences. The panel, titled "A Conversation on Privacy," was held at Centennial Hall and moderated by Nuala

O'Connor, CEO of the Center for Democracy and Technology. The speakers were Noam Chomsky, Glenn Greenwald, and, live-streaming from Russia, Edward Snowden himself. Carse was able to sit within a few dozen yards from legends and listen to Edward Snowden live. Crazy.

Back-to-back nights. Live events. Deep thinkers. With my sons.

Those two evenings changed how I think about technology. They shaped the way I understand screens and digital life. Technology is not morally neutral. Your digital self is an extension of your personhood, and both deserve protection, and privacy.

THE WORK

Take a digital Sabbath[2]

Take a digital sabbatical

Rest your human operating system.

Screen sanity:

spend less time in front of screens.

If you are using free social media

you are the product.[3]

Technology is not neutral.[4]

Keep your kids off technology

as long as you can

forever is the ideal.

Crush your screens

all of them

crush them.

Use Proton email for email.

Attention is the currency

of the digital age.

Unplug

to reconnect.

TAILBOARD: SOCIAL MEDIA AND NARRATIVES

Social Media

I want you to think about something. Think about the billions of people who have come before you in life and are now dead. Estimates are that ~100 million people have died due to communism. About 13 million people were killed in the Holocaust. There have been other genocides. Most of these people came and went with little fanfare, nobody knew them. Think of the poor peasant farmers around the world working in fields day and night to eke out a marginal existence. They will die and nobody will have heard of them.

Social media has turned our natural human instinct for social approval, to be a member of the tribe, into an evil end of manipulation. Do you think it's a mistake that your generation experiences anxiety and depression at rates unheard of in the history of humankind and correlate to the proliferation of social media and technology?[5]

Through no one's fault, because we simply did not know what social media companies were doing, you have now been conditioned from a young age to compare yourself to others on social media and seek group approval through Likes, Dislikes, and number of followers. And, likely, given the wiring of the human person, you perceive this as an existential threat to the core of your being.

Remember, evolutionarily speaking, a member exiled or ostracized from the tribe would surely die, as the tribe was needed for protection. So while technology has advanced rapidly, our poor human brain is still thousands of years behind and perceives threats when our posts are not liked on social media.

Yet, billions of people have come before us and died and nobody knew their names, despite Facebook and the Metaverse. While it is chilling to the core to think of a lonely death, are you able to realize that you are not that significant to the vast population, who doesn't know your name? Let it be said, your significance resides in you, your family, and your genuine close friendships. And while you play on social media, the only people who are actually significant in your lives, sit quietly by on the sidelines waiting to engage with you.

I implore you, if you have not already done so, to break away as much as you can from social media- any place that creates feedback loops where you must seek Likes and have followers. And I ask that you to continue to lean into friendships, romances, and time together with others.

I ask you to consider that you really are the Captain of your Ship, the Master of your Fate, and that you do have Free Will and self-agency. I use the word "Operator," to suggest that Operators don't wait to be influenced by their environment, they act to influence the environment to their liking. This is the essence of self-agency, we can influence our world with our actions. Our actions have tangible consequences in this world. If I pick up the axe and go to work on forcing entry on the front door of a house fire, through my physical work in an objective, material world, the door busts open. I did that. Me.

I was walking the dogs around the block with Grace yesterday and she asked me, "what is the meaning of life?" How does one answer that question?

My Dad, buried in Southern, Arizona, used to say, "Live, Love, and Learn." In fact, this is on his headstone. It was his mantra. I think he believed this was the meaning of life: to live a fully examined life (Aristotle), to love others and to be loved deeply by others (this is risky business, as we may get hurt), and to continuously learn and apply that learning in new and creative ways. Another mantra my Dad would say, his Montana roots shining through, is, "live and let live." Truly a libertarian phrase and right up there with the Ten Commandments.

In addition to my Dad's wisdom, I do believe in the Divine, the Sacred Depth, the Creative Mystery, God. I don't really know how to articulate the Divine, other than I know it when I see it and I know when Divine grace surrounds me. Typically, the Divine shows up in the mundane. As I sit here writing, three dogs sleeping by me, quiet house (mom and Grace out shopping), listening to James Young[6] play quietly in the background, and as I engage my thoughts and hope to creatively express them to you, this moment has a certain element of divinity to it and I am aware of it. I call this Grace. And I suppose that it is moments like these, layered one on top of the other over the course of a lifetime, that might add up to something extraordinary, something akin to a meaningful life well lived.

And above all, I believe we must have hope, even if it's rugged hope. This has been the message of those who have come before us, going through the most horrible conditions imaginable. Those who were most likely to survive genocide believed in the possibility of a better future, they held on to Hope that something better was not only possible but imminent.

In addition to hope, we need to resist when it's appropriate to do so. In resilience work, it's very often the case that those who resist abuse in some way, even if subtle, faired far better in life than those who did not resist. We're not going to beat social media companies, but small acts of resistance and defiance are important for your long-term health and wellbeing.

When I was a kid my dad gave me a t-shirt, it had a little field mouse standing on the ground flipping a hawk off that was swooping down to snatch him. The shirt read, "The last great act of defiance." I have no idea why my dad gave me this t-shirt, and it's strange that I remember it. And yet, it stuck, and here we are.

Combine Grace and Hope with small acts of resistance, belief in the Divine, and pair these up with some living, loving, and learning, and Bruh, we got ourselves something special.

I've been on this planet earth for over 50 years. In my years, this is the most messed up period of human existence I have experienced and lived through. All these things happening in society, politics, race relationships, and general tomfoolery, the propaganda, and massive overreach of the surveillance state, and lack of privacy in all things, is deeply troubling. I don't know if things will get better, I am not sure.

But I do know that it is how I choose to think about these world events and my ability (self-agency) to take even small acts of resistance, my willingness to hold out hope, that allow me to tolerate all of it and continue to be happy with this existence, my life. I want the same for each of you.

I am suggesting that you live in an objective, material world and you have free will and self-agency and are able to shape your environment to your liking, to some degree. You get to decide the meaning of your life. So, get off social media, engage in genuine relationships, set some goals, chase after your dreams, and live large.

And by all means, don't forget hope, grace, and resistance.

Narratives

You should be aware of how mainstream media and Big Tech narratives operate in your lives.

What is often missed in the mainstream media narrative is the fact that each person has individual agency and autonomy. In an ideal world with a proper understanding, each person is responsible for their own actions and the consequences of their actions. This is what it means to be a person with self-agency and directing your own actions toward desired ends.

Don't miss this, as the underlying assumption taken by most media today is that "somebody else made me do it," or "somebody else is responsible for my actions." Not true. You and you alone are responsible for your actions and the consequences of your actions and decisions. To suggest otherwise is to remove self-agency from the person and hand it to someone else.

In a democracy, even though we may dislike the speech we are hearing from another, this is the dichotomy of living in a free society where it is presumed people have self-agency and are responsible for their actions.

We all must be careful because tides turn. One day, there will be another political administration and narratives will shift. This is a timeless truth, what goes around comes around. So while one administration is celebrating, in four years or eight years, the tides may turn and there will be new narratives shaped, or old ones reshaped.

If you've not watched Noam Chomsky's brilliant Manufacturing Consent,[7] you need to do so. Chomsky, a UA professor and often cited as one of the brightest minds alive, states that the media collude together to create a narrative for society. Another way of saying this would be to ask yourself the question, "What does the media want me to think today?" and then review various media and scan headlines and stories across the internet and see what narrative is being shaped by the power structures. It's likely, the headlines will echo.

Consider manufactured consent. What are you being led to believe by the power structure and why? Remember, government as a general rule, wants to grow bigger and have a say into your life. And, as I have suggested elsewhere, government is probably not your best friend. How much government is enough? Just enough.

It's clear that mainstream media and big tech control the dominant narratives in society, often times influenced by current political administrations. There are other narratives of course, but they don't get the airtime. They don't sink in. They don't get repeated. They don't echo across mainstream headlines or the social media feed.

You are autonomous and you have self-agency. Nobody is making you do anything.

A free society requires that we hear perspectives we disagree with, even the ones that make us uncomfortable. That's part of what shapes strong minds. You don't have to agree with every voice, but you should be able to hear them and decide for yourself. That's how free people think. That's what it means to live with self-agency.

The mainstream media and Big tech are probably not your best friends and you should limit, to the degree possible, inputs into their ecosystem. You should, at the very least, understand how narratives are built and how they work.

CHAPTER 10
ECONOMIC & POLITICS

SITUATIONAL AWARENESS

I learned a lot about myself this summer, truly. I worked around my house daily, repairing, cleaning, and preparing it for the market. My children helped me, scrubbing baseboards, hauling rock, trimming trees, and more. Thanks to our hard work, we got a contract on our house within seven days and sold it for a solid market price. Without the effort we put in, there's no way it would have sold that quickly—or for that number.

So, who was in control of that future profit? We were. I didn't have a boss. I was my own boss. I worked on the house knowing that the more effort I put into it, the more potential I had for a good return. I worked within a budget and prioritized what needed repair: tile in the master bath, a new kitchen sink, fresh carpet, landscaping, backyard plants to add color and life. We cleaned. We minimized. And it all made a difference.

Working with my hands, on my own schedule, with direct control over the creative outcome, there was something really meaningful about that. It opened a new window in my mind: maybe this is something I'd enjoy doing again. Could I buy an old house and flip it for profit?

I don't have the full answer, but I take pride in what we accomplished.

Our house in Tucson sold quickly. We now officially live in Montana. This is home, for now. All of our important material items are here. We've landed.

THE WORK

Pay yourself first

twenty percent.

Protect your principal

put your savings to work.

There was a time and a place in my life

where I was so poor

all I had was money.[1]

Money is a means

not an end.

The function of an automobile

is to get you safely from point A to point B.

Form follows function.

. . .

Minimize monthly payments

try not to have any.

Buy low

sell high.

Simple common sense

but easier said than done.

Albert Einstein was once asked

what mankind's greatest invention was.

He replied "Compound interest."

Some say he even called it

the eighth wonder of the world.[2]

Invest in your company's stock purchasing options.

Don't hurt people

don't take their stuff.[3]

That government is best

which governs least.[4]

. . .

How much government is enough?

Just enough.

Anarchy burger

hold the government, please.[5]

Government serves a purpose,

but requires

watchful attention.

Consider where your taxes flow

and what they truly build.

Some see necessity,

others see burden.

A balance worth contemplating.

War is a racket.[6]

Know where your taxes go.

Where do your state, federal, city, county

real estate, and income taxes go?

What are you paying for?

Do you see

if you have a reasonable income

and you minimize your expenses

and you take on little debt

and you reduce your taxes

and you put your money to work

this is how wealth is built.

It takes money to make money.

Have three to six months financial reserves

in the bank

in high yield savings.

Ladder certificates of deposit.

Avoid debt

limit taxes

put your money to work

in a socially responsible

manner.

Bank at local credit unions.

Live within your means.

There are two ways to be rich

one: by acquiring much

the other by desiring little.[7]

Understand what opportunity cost is.

This idea, this concept

can be used throughout your life

in various settings.

Real estate triangle:

location, price, house.

You only get two sides of the triangle.

Consider a middle path

between individual freedom

and collective care.

Neither wholly one nor the other

but a mindful balance

where both can breathe.[8]

When lending to family

your children

avoid charging interest.

Money between loved ones

creates its own currency

of care and obligation.

Keep these waters clear

and free from the marketplace.

Support your local mom and pop shops.

Buy an older, smaller house

a fixer-upper

as close as possible

to the best ranked public school in the area.

Communism has killed

a lot of people.

The dream and the doing

are different things.

Some socialist tendencies

schools, roads, care for the poor

these have been good.

But absolute power

corrupts absolutely.

Watch the documentary Manufactured Consent[9]

by Noam Chomsky.

Manufactured consent is a powerful process.

TPTB = the powers that be.

Speak truth to power

The powers that be.

If you go into a pub in Ireland

there are two topics you don't talk about:

politics and religion.

This is good advice for life.

TAILBOARD: MODERN WALDEN: URBAN EDITION AND MONK OR MILLIONAIRE

Modern Walden: Urban Edition

Recently, my second-born son Carse, and by far my most creative child, was involved in a T-bone car accident in Tempe, Arizona. Carse took a full-sized truck smack dab into the driver's side door of his small, four-door sedan.

Thankfully, Carse was not injured in the accident, and neither was his brother, Coop, who was riding shotgun in the passenger seat. The car exploded the side-curtain and front airbags and protected them both as the breakaway frame of the car absorbed the energy of the accident. In this instance, modern technology was a sweet blessing.

The accident clearly rattled Carse. He showed up to his parents' house later that evening, and it was clear he was shook. After many years on the fire department, I know what rattled looks and feels like, and I could tell Carse was experiencing adrenaline and emotions. I suppose most of us, when we have a brush with our mortality, pause and reflect on life and shake at what could have been.

Even on a great day, a normal day, Carse is an interesting character. He graduated from Arizona State University in May 2020 with a Bachelor of Science degree from ASU's Herberger Institute for Design and the Arts. Carse's love of art likely stems from an inner predisposition toward the arts, yes, but also from an exceptional art teacher he had while in elementary school. As the salty father of four children, and with many years of parent-teacher interactions under my belt, I still marvel at the impact great teachers have on the lives of their students.

Unfortunately, Carse was not able to attend 2020 graduation ceremonies at ASU due to the COVID-19 global pandemic. ASU suspended ceremonies and opted for online commencement. What an auspicious start to a new life following four years of academic persistence.

I often wonder how this lack of closure and formal transition to a new beginning has—and may continue to—affect Carse and many in his generation. I worry because every society across the horizon of time and in different cultures has rites of passage, including graduation ceremonies, to help members of the community transition well to new phases of life. Were it me, I would create my own commencement ceremony and ensure closure and a new beginning from my time in college and toward my new, adult life afterward.

At my parents' house, we hugged it out, shed a few tears, and calmed nerves with relaxing pool time, beers, a home-cooked meal, and a good movie on the couch to end the night.

Within a few days after the accident, we learned the insurance company was totaling the car, claiming it more expensive to repair than it would be to replace. Carse quickly received payment from our insurance company on the equity in his car, and they paid off the remaining balance of his loan to the finance company. Carse now has a fair amount of money sitting in his bank account as he explores buying a new sedan to replace his car.

For the past six years, Carse has lived in downtown Tempe, Arizona, close to all of the activity one would expect in a large university city. ASU, which sits in the middle of Tempe—and, in fact, defines Tempe—is one of the world's largest university systems. Because Carse is an architect with an interest in urban planning, as cities go, he is in an environment that mirrors his studies, his interests, and his future plans.

On a normal day, I think about my children and their lives often. When big events—like car accidents—happen, I find myself investing even more time and attention to deep thought on their behalf.

After Carse's accident, I was thinking a lot about him and his life and this situation. The most immediate line of thinking was about a new car for Carse and quickly renewing his means of transportation. I was thinking about best models of cars (form follows function), financing, interest rates, increased car prices due to low supply, high demand, and disrupted supply chain logistics.

I was on a walk, on a Saturday morning, doing my best creative thinking on behalf of Carse, knowing full well he probably doesn't much care what I think. This is the nature of being the father to a self-reliant 24-year-old son who did three years of hard time in a frat at ASU.

I spent years investing my life into Carse's life, and then one day I gave him a smartphone when he turned 13. Then, almost overnight, he went to college. Now, it's hard to connect with Carse in a meaningful way given the vicissitudes of life; "Cats in the Cradle" be damned. As a father, it's been a brutal and painful grieving process for me, losing my children one by one from our nest to a culture that I cannot fight against and win.

As I walked and processed and got lost in my Sabbath ambulation, the new line of thinking that was coming to me was—what if Carse did not purchase a new car to replace his lost car, and he made a decision not to own a car?

It's easy to see that almost all American cities are built around cars and vehicles, rather than around people and gathering spaces. It's also easy to see many European cities do very well without vehicles crammed into their inner core.

In 1999, I was in Stockholm, Sweden, and I will never forget how beautiful the women were. They were lean and fit and they glowed. Through observation and conversation, it became clear that this was the case because people walked and biked to their destinations, or they took local transportation, like buses. There were very few cars.

This was the same story when I visited friends in Geneva, Switzerland, in 2010. My friends, to this day, do not own a car, and they have lived in Geneva for 15 years working for the World Health Organization.

In America, we are pudgy and out of shape. We are dependent upon vehicles. We are conditioned by the culture we live in and the advertising and marketing—psychological manipulation—that goes into nudging us, consumers, to buy cars.

We are shaped from a very early age with tidal waves of marketing surrounding us to be "consumers." That smartphone has, and continues to do, its work.

Nevertheless, in a small act of defiance and resistance, and in honor of caring about our planet, I believe it's possible for Carse to thumb his nose at the exploitative, non-generative system we live in and NOT purchase a new car!

Carse lives in downtown Tempe, a mile from his work, and everything he does is almost always within the Tempe area.

With a combination of light rail, Uber, ride-sharing, walking, biking, renting a car when necessary, and carpooling with friends, I think it's entirely possible Carse could live well in Tempe without a vehicle. Further, many grocery stores now deliver groceries.

Between savings on car insurance, a car payment, gasoline, regular maintenance and repair on a vehicle, a substantial savings could be realized, and this money could be saved and later invested into an asset that actually appreciates in value.

I imagine being without a car would make your world seem smaller. Certainly, the two-mile radius around you would become more intimate. But perhaps true community, once we narrow our traveling distance, is to be found as we live, move, work, and play closer to home.

In America, we equate cars with freedom. This is most certainly an emotional state, but nevertheless, it's a real psychological phenomenon that one would have to contend with.

Can a 24-year-old young man break the familiar mold and live a more creative life outside the system? I don't know, fully, but I do see this as an opportunity to experiment as a modern-day Walden.

As I think about giving up the privilege of owning a car, the biggest negative I can think of is the increased danger of walking and biking in traffic, as hundreds of bicyclists die each year being struck by distracted drivers.

Our cityscapes are not built for pedestrians; they are built for cars, and this is the real tragedy.

It's clear that as the father of four children, three of them twenty-something, I can't tell them what to do. But as a dad, I can experiment with the idea, on behalf of Carse, about opting out of vehicle ownership for a season of life and unshackling from the Car Manufacturer–Petro–Finance–Insurance Industrial Complex.

In fact, it may be the case that I, too, have to unshackle from my own vehicle for a season of life.

. . .

Monk or Millionaire

Coop and I have a little saying: "Monk or Millionaire." It means, if you're going to engage the system in America—the Matrix—you might as well play the game and play hard and go for that million dollars. Or, conversely, you might see the wisdom in opting out of the system, or recognizing that the system is inherently rigged against the average man, and become a monk. (Incidentally, I don't see monk or millionaire as zero-sum or mutually exclusive. I do believe one could be both—or, further, become a millionaire and then a monk, or vice versa.)

In the end, the world's average salary is around $20,000 a year (depending on exchange rates and country data). The median household income in the U.S. is approximately $75,000 as of the latest census.

Here's a quote: "The ideal income point for individuals is $95,000 for life satisfaction and $60,000 to $75,000 for emotional well-being. When people earned more than $105,000, their happiness levels decreased."

I have been working in the same profession—fire service—for most of my life. I am not rich, never have been, and likely never will be. But I can say with integrity, I am happy with my life and the life I have lived. It's been honest and in service to others. I've worked for the government, in all jobs, and my motive has always been service instead of profit margin. I don't know what it's like to work for a for-profit company, a private employer. I've not had that experience.

What I am seeing in my children is that my lessons in money over the years have paid off. I am proud of all my children. They are doing well.

By the way, I really don't care how much money my children make. I want them to be happy and successful. When I say successful, that means however they would define it. But John Wooden says this about success: "Success is peace of mind that is the direct result of self-satisfaction in knowing you did your best to become the best that you are capable of becoming."

Now if I can just get my children to embrace their spiritual lives and lean in toward a belief system. Having a belief system is normative and important for happiness in life. Judaism, Buddhism, Taoism, Christianity, Islam, Agnostic, Atheist, New Age Spirituality, etc.

Keep in mind, there are better belief systems than others—but that's their work to figure out. If they are like me, their belief system will probably become more important in their life around the time they are going to have their first child.

Then, things will get real.

———

CHAPTER 11
WORK

SITUATIONAL AWARENESS

After ten years on the fire department, I was feeling it. I was working at busy fire stations, and I was burnt out. My wife was feeling it too. Neither of us liked living in the city, it wasn't where we wanted to raise our two young sons, two and four at the time.

So, we came up with a plan. We decided we were both going to go back to school and become certified teachers. The idea was to spend a year living in family housing at Northern Arizona University, earn our teaching credentials, and then move to a remote area of Alaska to teach in indigenous communities, as a husband-and-wife team.

We wrote it all out. We made a plan and started working through it. Step by step, item by item, we crossed things off our list—month after month. Finally, we reached the last step: sell the house, resign our jobs, and move.

We sold the house in seven days. And we freaked out.

We lost our nerve. We looked at our two little boys and wondered what we were thinking, resigning from stable jobs in a shaky world. We pulled back. We moved into a rental. A few months later, we bought a new house, and lived there for many years.

Fast forward to 2019. We made a different kind of move, this time to Montana, to a much smaller city. My wife became a public school teacher. I became a faculty member at the university, teaching fire science and outdoor adventure leadership. Not all, but many of our students were American Indian.

We didn't make it to Alaska. But the dream changed us anyway. I'm grateful for the work my hands have been given in this life.

THE WORK

Work was before

the fall of man

in the Garden of Eden and after the fall.

Man has to work.

Early to bed, early to rise makes a man healthy

wealthy

and wise.[1]

Success is peace of mind

that is the direct result of self-satisfaction in knowing

you did your best to become

the best that you

are capable of becoming.[2]

Do not take the time to answer your non-constructive critics.

Where the needs of this world and your passions intersect

this is your occupation and career.[3]

Take several personality and behavioral assessments

like the Myers-Briggs.[4]

Use them as tools and guides.

These assessments are descriptive, not prescriptive.

Don't let the results paint you into a corner

use them as guides.

You work to support your family

your family is not there to support your work.

Follow through

Pay attention to detail

Stickiness.

.   .   .

Keep a three-ring portfolio binder

organize your work life inside it:

certificates, résumés, awards

letters of recommendation, and more.

Work:

Work hard

Do the work

Be on time—better yet, early

Stay late

Get along with your peers

Support your boss and the organization

Contribute

Be a good team player

Treat customers well.

Generally speaking

support labor unions.

I remember talking to a marine biologist

on a research ship in the harbor of San Diego.

She stood on the balcony of the boat

salt in the air

sunshine on her face

the ocean all around.

She didn't make a lot of money

but she loved her work

She was happy.

Pursue happiness

Pursue bliss

The rest will follow.

The art of the start:

Sometimes, you just have to start.

Sometimes, you don't need A-level work out of the gate.

Sometimes, B and C+ level work is sufficient

start with that

refine as you go.

My favorite job was being a Fire Science instructor at MSUB.

It was my lowest-paying job

but I loved my students

loved teaching

relished my time off.

Four months off over summer

one month off over winter break

plus spring and fall breaks.

Balance.

TAILBOARD: REFLECTIONS ON WORK

Life as a House

It's about 9 a.m., and the kids are still sleeping. Victoria went for a walkabout. I am having a cup of java, catching up on morning email, and now, writing.

I bought a favorite movie at the used bookstore recently titled Life as a House.[5] If you've not seen it, check it out—it's on my top ten list. Oh, I don't know why, it just is, and I like the flavor of the movie, the pacing, the story.

The quick synopsis is that a man works as an architect for over 20 years but more or less dislikes his job. Throughout these years, he has lived in a house near the beach that is a tiny crackerbox. He's had plans to remodel and rebuild a new house, but as of yet has not. He gets fired from his job and then diagnosed with terminal cancer. He pre-advances his life insurance and sets to building his dream house before he dies.

Meanwhile, he is a divorcé with a son, and his son is having major problems. He brings his troubled son to live with him for the summer, and the two of them together build the house. That's the story.

A little over a year ago, a woman I work with lost a battle with metastatic breast cancer. I used to sit in and chat with her, about nothing really, when I stopped by the administrative offices.

She really disliked her job and could not wait to retire. Yet, she died in the job she disliked and never was able to build her house.

Is it not true that we are all building a house? Think about this for a moment. In the back of your mind, don't you picture some different life, and different way of living, a different and altogether meaningful life?

For example, I know at least one of you really would move to Europe tomorrow if given the possibility. Some dream of living in the mountains, in a wooden cabin with a red brick fireplace heating the home. Others, like me, perhaps a small cottage by the ocean. Some want to travel to Europe for months. Others want to hike the Appalachian Trail in its entirety. Cruise around the world, sail the seas, visit Anne Frank's house in Amsterdam, make a pilgrimage to Lumbini, Nepal.

Mentally, if not spiritually, we are all building a house. A few lucky souls have already built theirs, and they are living in it.

My question is, why do we wait to actually build our house? Why does it have to be a mental house in the recess of our mind, and not an actual "house" that we build each day? Is life that bland, that we really are bound to the jobs we dislike, in environments we don't like, simply to survive?

God, the Divine, the Sacred Mystery, has set a house in our hearts. I know He has mine. And I think we have an obligation to build the darn thing.

Descent

Descent is the term I use that asks us to consider the entire trip during our life, both climbing up and going down. What follows is a reflection.

I woke up this morning, as I usually do, to my dogs stretching over me and licking my face. We have two Shihtzus and one Maltese-Bichon mix, a rescue. They are my pals. It's 6:00 a.m., and they are ready to walk around the block. It's what we do.

I'm learning from my dogs to stretch long and deep before I get out of bed. It seems like a healthy practice. One way that I know I am relaxed is to feel that long, deep stretch in the morning. When I am stressed, the stretch is not there, I can't find it.

On my mind this morning, for whatever reason, is Mount Everest. I no longer question why thoughts and memories and future planning surface, I simply accept that they are there, and it is what it is. So this is how thinking about Mt. Everest is.

I am wondering about the death rates climbing Mt. Everest versus descending Mt. Everest. Perhaps I am on this line of thought because I am interested in the long-view of life. There used to be a fascinating blog, that I can no longer find nor name, that posted about "the long-view." I am not talking about a few years out, but hundreds of years out.

How many of us take an eternal perspective of life and think about how our thoughts, words, and deeds will manifest in hundreds, thousands, millions of years? Eternity? What action am I taking today that is shaping the person I will become tomorrow, and into eternity?

I get the dogs around the block, hug and kiss my wife and kids as they head off to school, and rest in the grace of being and expressing love. A bit weird, that sentence, coming from a man—touching into emotion like that. But after my career, knowing how fragile life can be, what's there to lose?

After everyone is gone, out the door, I begin my morning three-mile walk. As I am praying the Lord's Prayer, it begins to rain. This motivates me to jog, and I jog at a medium pace as the rain drizzles down. It's perfect. A morning baptism, and I need it.

I get home and begin my morning meditation. I set my timer for 20 minutes. A few minutes in, the rain deepens, gets heavy, and comes down in buckets. It rains cats and dogs, I can hear them thud as they hit my roof. This makes for a beautiful meditation on sound, and I simply rest in the sound of rain coming down.

Here I am typing, and I know the answer. I just looked it up. Fifteen percent of climbers that have died on Mt. Everest died climbing up. The rest, 85%, died coming down, during descent.

I'm not going to go off on a long tangent here, but consider how society, culture, shapes the modern-day worker. Young men and women are encouraged—demanded—to climb up. Education, work hard, promotion, training, work hard, prove yourself, promotion—climb up. In a word, striving.

But the workplace, in most instances, does not take into consideration your descent. My observation here, and understanding my own past history, is that each of us has the responsibility to take the long-view of life and consider, especially in the working world, our descent. It's the descent that kills climbers.

It's a good morning. My dogs are at my feet, I am expressing myself in writing, and the rain continues to fall.

I am content to just be.

CHAPTER 12
SAFETY

SITUATIONAL AWARENESS

I n the early 1970s, perfectly sound commercial aircraft were crashing at unprecedented rates. Investigations uncovered that airplanes were not crashing due to mechanical failure, but because of human behavior in the cockpit.

At the time, the private airline industry was loaded with retired military fighter pilots. Like my peers in the fire department, fighter pilots brought their bravado and egos into the cultural environment of flying commercial airplanes. The pilot was not to be questioned or challenged. Teamwork was not a cultural norm.

But all people, at all times, are prone to error. To err is human.[1] The real challenge is that when I am in error, I usually do not know it. I can't see it by myself.

Born from those airline tragedies was a training program titled Crew Resource Management (CRM). Early adopters will remember CRM as "Charm School." It's funny, isn't it, how anytime the notion of human behavior or emotional intelligence is brought up in male-dominated professions, it gets labeled "Charm

School"? Yet it's within these human dynamics where accidents, injuries, and our greatest blind spots reside.

At its foundation, CRM is about team. It asserts that it takes all members of a team to land the mission safely. All resources, especially human resources, are brought to bear.

Once CRM becomes a cultural norm, it makes it "okay" to professionally question leaders, with the understanding that leaders, too, have blind spots. It takes the full crew, not just the person with the title, to navigate the mission safely.

Shortly after CRM was implemented, the number of airline crashes dropped significantly.

THE WORK

Never drink and drive

don't get in the car as a passenger

with someone who has been drinking and is driving

or is otherwise under the influence.

Wear a seatbelt.

Look both ways

before clearing an intersection.

Have operable smoke detectors

in every room and hallway of your house.

Have CO detectors on every level of your house.

Keep your house well lit at night.

There really are bad people
out there
avoid them.

Trust your gut
your gut is wired to your brain.

Drink in moderation.

Most fatalities on Mount Everest
happen during descent.[2]

Three to go, one no-go.
In helicopter life flights
all three crew members
have to feel good about the flight
if even one crew member is uncomfortable
it's a no-go.[3]

. . .

Fentanyl is everywhere.

When you go out

don't take things

offered by other people.

If you must have firearms

store them properly

locked

unloaded

ammunition stored separately.

It's not just safety

it's responsibility.

Never, never, never

leave young children

unattended

near water.

Bathtubs, buckets, pools, ponds

drowning is silent

and it happens fast.

. . .

There is safety in numbers

There is safety in others

Go out with friends and stay together.

Two by two

Jesus sent them.[4]

TAILBOARD: RISK MANAGEMENT AND POSITIVE MENTAL ATTITUDE

My fire department career was not without risk. Each year, about 100 firefighters died in the line of duty. The mission of the fire department is straightforward, protect life and property in the community. Sometimes, to protect life, firefighters must put their own lives in harm's way.

We didn't throw ourselves willy-nilly into dangerous situations. Each incident was approached methodically. The "risk management profile" that guided most of my fire department life has seeped into my everyday life, and I want to share it with you, because I believe it's a useful tool for navigating life's risks.

Here's how we thought about it:

- We will risk our lives a lot, in a highly calculated manner, to save savable lives.
- We will risk our lives a little, in a highly calculated manner, to save savable property.
- We will not risk our lives at all to save that which is already lost.

I've used this profile when making decisions that involve risk in my personal life. For example, traveling 6,200 miles with my family to a foreign country to serve in short-term international aid work. After doing our research, talking with others, praying, planning, and preparing, we took the risk. It was highly calculated, and it was worth it.

By contrast, I've never jumped out of an airplane or gone bungee jumping. Not because I'm afraid, but because, to me, those activities present unnecessary risk. There's nothing to save. Life is already full of risk, why add more for the sake of a thrill?

I'm not saying you shouldn't do those things. I'm just saying they don't make sense to me in my risk-reward calculus. If you go, I'll cheer you on from the ground.

There's a book called Do Hard Things: A Teenage Rebellion Against Low Expectations, by Alex Harris. One of its main ideas is that we should do hard things in life that have deep meaning. That sounds right to me. It sounds like risking a lot, in a highly calculated manner, to save savable lives.

So yes, take risks. But take meaningful, calculated ones. Let your risks offer something better to the world.

Don't put it all on the line every day, or even often. And if you ever feel tempted to go all in, to put all your chips on the table and risk everything you've worked for on a single roll of the dice, don't. Step back. Sleep on it. Return with more clarity.

There's a story that's stayed with me. Researchers once asked a group of centenarians—people over 100 years old—what they regretted most. The most common answer? That they had played it too safe. That they wished they had taken more risks.

That stuck with me. It still does.

But there's another layer here. There's more to life than risk management. Life throws you into unpredictable situations. Plans fail. Pressure mounts. Things fall apart. In those moments, you need something else—a kind of internal ballast. A mindset.

A Positive Mental Attitude (PMA).

I learned about this through Search & Rescue training. When we talk about survival in the wilderness, what separates those who live from those who don't, it's not always skill, gear, or physical strength. It's PMA. The will to live. The mindset to adapt and move forward.

Positive self-talk, setting small goals, making the situation into a mental game, these are the tools that help people survive when lost or stranded or afraid. I've used them myself. In rescue scenarios, I sometimes detach slightly, focus on the task, and work my way through. Step by step. Patient by patient. It becomes a kind of game. A way to move forward when things get rough.

That's not just survival in the woods. That's life.

Right now, we're facing uncertainty. Economically, politically, culturally, everything's shifting. There's fear in the air. But we don't need to panic. We need to adapt.

Darwin didn't say the strongest survive. He said those who adapt survive. That's our work, learning to live well in changing realities. Being willing to revise our mental models, adjust our habits, and keep moving forward.

Part of that is practical. Stock some food and water. Fill your gas tank. Keep cash at home. Don't hoard, but prepare. Have first aid supplies and dog food and a flashlight. Live wisely.

Part of that is mental. Practice good situational awareness. Ask "what if" questions, not to spiral into anxiety, but to think through your next moves in various situations. Run the OODA loop: Observe, Orient, Decide, Act.

Breathe. Adjust. Return to the loop and act again.

And part of that is spiritual. Keep a positive outlook. Pray. Meditate. Laugh. Play music. Sit in the sun. Call your friends. Hug your kids. Pet the dog. Cry if you need to. Watch the weather. Listen to the rain. Know your risk. Trust your mind. Find your footing. Live prepared. Stay grateful. Then get up and keep going.

And always, always, keep a positive mental attitude.

———

CHAPTER 13
LEARNING

SITUATIONAL AWARENESS

One of the best learning environments I've ever been in was at Phoenix Community College, taking a course titled Medical and Biological Ethics, taught by Dr. O'Brien.

Dr. O'Brien was a retired Dominican priest of the Roman Catholic Church. He had received permission from the Church to marry a nun, and the rest, as they say, was history. He had ten children. Yes, ten. And he lived a good, honest life.

There weren't many students in the class, but Dr. O'Brien rained down lightning when he lectured. Have you ever heard a Dominican lecture? His eyes would close softly, and then, his verbal cylinders fired wide open. He filled us with a knowledge of what is true, beautiful, and good in this world.

There's a story I remember him telling. He said a university president had died, and hundreds attended the funeral. It was a big event, a flash-bang affair. Apparently, there's something about a dead university president worth celebrating.

Around the same time, the university landscaper died, a Hispanic man who had worked the grounds for nearly 30 years. No one heard about or knew he died. The funeral was small, lightly attended.

Dr. O'Brien created a learning environment where I learned to think—really think—about loyal Hispanic men with small funerals, and university presidents with flash-bang big ones.

THE WORK

All learning is self-learning

Always be reading and learning.

The man who knows he doesn't know... knows.[1]

The more you know

the less you know.[2]

Nobody can ever take away

your education

or your knowledge.[3]

Seek first to understand

then to be understood.[4]

. . .

A learning objective has four parts:

A condition

The learning to take place

Behavior

Performance level

A good lesson plan should only have

three to five learning objectives

no more

no less.

I hear and I forget

I see and I remember

I do and I understand.[5]

How to learn:

See one

Do one

Teach one.

How to teach:

Let them see one

Do one

Teach one.

A single conversation

across the table with a wise man

is worth

a month's study of books.

Change the story

change the world.

Language is powerful.

Writing is the closest thing we have to real magic.[6]

Give a man a fish, you feed him for a day.

Teach a man to fish, you feed him for a lifetime.[7]

How do you teach a man to fish?

I do, you watch (see one)

I do, you help (do one)

You do, I help (do one)

You do, I watch (teach one)[8]

The root word of disciple is learner, or follower.
In discipline, the goal is to educate and teach
not to hurt.

Discipline = learning.
When we discipline a child
or a subordinate at work
the purpose is learning
a new behavior.

We only know
that learning has occurred
when we observe
a change in behavior.

Education = visible change in behavior.
Learning = visible change in behavior.

The number one predictor
of a child's academic success

is the education level of the mother.

Be teachable
Be willing to learn.

Montessori is an exceptional
educational methodology.

If your kids want to go to
boat-building school in Norway
or furniture-making school in Maine
instead of traditional college
let them.

There is nothing wrong with homeschooling.

People earn more money over a lifetime
with a college degree.

Consider getting your master's degree
it's not required for success
or for more money

but it won't hurt.

Study and understand propaganda.

Notice

there is no college course titled Propaganda 101.

Why?

There's no education on the methods of propaganda

in grade school or high school either.

Why?

Consider that

think about it.

Read Edward Bernays' work on propaganda.[9]

Reading a book

is one of the highest-leverage activities on earth.

You do yourself a disservice

by not reading.

Be thoughtful and considerate

of other perspectives.

Learn why someone believes what they do.

TAILBOARD: TOWARD MASTERY- A PHILOSOPHY OF TRAINING AND LEARNING

What follows is a developing philosophy of training, specifically within the fire service. But if you're not a firefighter, don't tune out. This isn't just about fire. It's about learning, mastery, and high performance under pressure. The tools and approaches here apply to any domain where the stakes are high, the pace is fast, and the need for continuous improvement is real.

Training, and learning, should reach all members of the fire department. This includes field personnel as well as administrative staff.

For staff and administrative teams, I envision two primary outcomes: learn something and build team. Nothing more, and nothing less.

For operations personnel, our firefighters, the focus of training must be basic skills, leading toward mastery. It's the lack of basic skills that injures or kills firefighters. The foundational skills are not glamorous, but they're everything. Air management. SCBA use. Search and rescue. Forcible entry. Ventilation. Apparatus placement. Hose lays. Hose streams. Correct line placement and advancement.

Seventy-five percent of our training time should focus on these basics. The remaining twenty-five percent? Response to downed firefighters: Rapid Intervention Training (RIT).

But let me be clear, no amount of RIT training can replace sound decision-making on the fireground. Strong command presence, correct strategies and tactics, and real-time evaluation of the Incident Action Plan will prevent more injuries than any RIT class we ever teach.

Training should be hands-on, realistic, and stress-inoculated. It should be repetitive and progression-based. We train as we perform. Under stress, people don't rise to the occasion, they fall to their level of training.

We must build correct neural circuits on the front end.

Consider this: police officers have been found dead with spent brass casings in their hands. Why? Because in training they were taught to pick up their brass. That habit stuck. It imprinted. Even under life-threatening pressure.

This is why training design matters. Not just the content, but the delivery platform. Some topics, like bench grinder safety, can be handled online. Others, like air management, must be hands-on. Crawl, walk, run. Over and over.

Company officers must take training seriously. Every firefighter must recognize the value of lifelong learning. This is not optional.

And we must also go deeper.

After three days in a human performance course taught by Navy SEALs, one thing became very clear: mental performance is just as critical as physical skill, if not more. What makes SEALs elite isn't just physical strength. It's mindset. Breath control. Mental rehearsal. Meditation.

The SEALs, arguably the most elite fighters on earth, train their minds. They walk through scenarios in their heads long before stepping onto the battlefield. This is why they stay calm under fire. Combat becomes second nature.

This must be part of our training environments too.

Mental rehearsal, breathwork, and stress inoculation belong in our training environments. We must build calm, focused minds that know how to respond with clarity under pressure.

Likewise, we must integrate high impact practices (HIPs) that encourage collaboration and deeper engagement. In a fire service that still lacks diversity, these practices matter. They help create a culture of listening, of valuing other perspectives, which leads to greater safety, both in the firehouse and on the fireground.

Here's one example: have crews work together on a live fire behavior project. Build scaled-down wooden houses—"dollhouses." Light them. Observe. Learn. Debrief. Collaborate. Let firefighters talk it through, share predictions, test ideas, and explain what they see.

This kind of hands-on, high-engagement learning creates buy-in. It also builds the habit of seeing through multiple lenses, and that's how safety cultures grow.

And just as important, we need continuous learning loops. Not just one-time trainings, but habits of reflection that build over time. One of the best tools for this is the After Action Review (AAR).

AARs are simple. They ask:

1. What was the plan?
2. What happened?
3. Why did it happen?
4. What will we do differently next time?

I've done them professionally and personally. After college semesters. After job interviews. After family situations. The reflection makes the next version better.

The SEALs also use a tight AAR format:

- What are our three sustains?
- What are our three improves?

Pick the version that works. But use it. Build the habit. Get 1% better every day.

Too often, fire department training divisions are under-resourced. That must change, because training is not a side project. It is the job.

I'd like to see more fire department training divisions lead professional development across their organizations, not just for firefighters, but for everyone. The ripple effects on the community could be massive.

A back-to-the-basics approach, grounded in safety, learning from mistakes, mental performance, and continuous review, is not just effective. It's essential.

This is how we grow.

And all of it must lead—ultimately—toward mastery.[10]

———

CHAPTER 14
LEADERSHIP

SITUATIONAL AWARENESS

On the fire department, I remember working under two assistant chiefs. One was absolutely dialed when it came to getting work done. He had an MBA, was analytical, and made decisions rooted in data. The guy got things done, and done well. But the challenge? He didn't work well with people, especially the rank and file firefighters. He operated with a Theory X mindset, he believed most people were lazy, unmotivated, and in constant need of supervision.

The second chief? Beloved. Especially by the firefighters. He was warm, friendly, family-oriented, easy to be around. All good leadership qualities. The challenge? He didn't move the needle in the organization. He didn't drive change. Data and results weren't really on his radar.

Watching those two chiefs shaped me. I realized I wanted balance. I wanted to lead from a framework that valued both the mission and the people. I wanted to be effective, mission-driven, data-aware, moving the organization forward, and at the same time, I wanted to be approachable, grounded, and kind.

Be worker-centered. Be people-first. But don't forget: we have a mission. We have a job to do. That's the approach that's stuck with me.

THE WORK

Things are not always black and white

learn how to lead (and live) in the grey

leadership is the ability to work through grey.

The higher you climb

the more grey (ambiguity) you face

black and white is easy

grey is not.

Observe

Orient

Decide

Act

(OODA).[1]

Loop this over and over again

every day, all day

observe, orient, decide, act.

.   .   .

Analyze

Plan

Implement

Evaluate

(APIE).[2]

A hazardous materials framework

use it in decision-making.

Conduct After Action Reviews (AARs) often

they tighten the learning cycle

leading to better decisions and outcomes.

After Action Review:[3]

What was my plan?

What happened?

Why did it happen?

What will I do differently next time?

Leadership equals influence[4]

nothing more, nothing less.

. . .

Leadership is a choice

not a position.

Slow is smooth

smooth is fast.

Efficiency reduces effort.

Vision + ethics + courage + reality = leadership.

Captivating the emotions of others = leadership.

One of the best leadership books is:

Primal Leadership.[5]

Leadership is behavior

that can be observed.[6]

Leaders are made.

How?

Disciplined intention

Education

Training

Experience

Failure + Recovery

Mentoring.

Character:

Your thoughts become your words

Your words become your actions

Your actions become your habits

Your habits become your character

Your character becomes your destiny.

Be mindful of your thoughts

guard them.[7]

Most athletes, including firefighters

focus on the physical

but the real game

is mental.

Mindset matters

have a growth mindset.

        . . .

Leadership is a set of skills that can be learned

over time, those skills create synergy

they compound

they influence

they can be observed.

SMART goals:[8]

Specific

Measurable

Attainable

Realistic

Timed.

'Towering competence' is

what I expected from firefighters

when I was a captain and battalion chief.

How much leadership is enough?

Just enough.

In leadership and supervision

praise is often harder to give

than reprimands.

Leadership = learning.

Leadership = connecting hearts to the work.

How?

Face time

Storytelling

Legend and lore

Get their hearts involved.

Fireground levels:

Strategic – Chiefs

Tactical – Captains

Task – Firefighters.

Leaders work strategically

not at the task level

organizational gravity

pulls you downward

fight that pull.

You can't do it all

and you're not expected to.

Prioritize

and delegate.

In essentials, consistency

in non-essentials, liberty

in all things, unity.

I wouldn't give a fig for the simplicity

on the near side of complexity

but I would give my right arm

for the simplicity on the far side.[9]

Breathe

even in leadership

breathe.

DWYSYWD = Do What You Say You Will Do.

This builds trust

and trust is the foundation of every relationship.

You may not be able to change the culture

but you can change the immediate climate.

Leaders eat last[10]
lead from the point of the spear
be a servant leader.

Respect is a paradox
you must give it to receive it.

The fire department excels at:
Response
Operations
Problem-solving
The fire department struggles with:
Prevention
Education
Long-term thinking
Community risk reduction
Systems thinking

Where there is no vision
the people perish.[11]

. . .

Be brief

be bright

be gone.

Don't bring your boss problems

bring them solutions.

Concept: Move it to the right.

Visualize a continuum

sometimes you won't get the full outcome

but you can make small gains.

Move the needle

bite and hold.

At 211°, water is hot

At 212°, water boils.

One degree makes all the difference.

10,000 hours of practice = mastery.

That's 3 hours/day for 9 years

2 hours/day for 13.7

1 hour/day for 27.

Grab 15

one topic

15 minutes a day

for one year.

Read, watch, listen

grow.

Navy SEAL After Action Review (AAR):[12]

3 improves?

3 sustains?

A simple, powerful loop for continuous learning.

Don't play devil's advocate

be a "loyal opponent."[13]

Language matters.

Team (and family) development:

Forming

Storming

Norming

Performing

Be an Operator

influence your environment

don't wait to be influenced.

Sheep. Wolves. Sheepdogs.[14]

Sheep: kind, oblivious people

Wolves: predators

Sheepdogs: quiet warriors

who protect;

always watching the tree line.

"Out of every one hundred men,

ten shouldn't even be there,

eighty are just targets,

nine are the real fighters,

and we are lucky to have them,

for they make the battle.

But the one,

the one is a warrior—

and he will bring the others back."[15]

. . .

BHAGs: Big, Hairy, Audacious Goals.[16]

Ask yourself:

Am I investing in myself?

Am I genuinely interested in others?

Am I doing what I love—and loving what I do?

Am I spending time with the right people?

Am I staying in my strength zone?

Am I taking others to a higher level?

Am I taking care of today?

Am I taking time to think?

Am I developing others?

Am I pleasing God?[17]

Trust is the foundation of any team.

How to gain trust:

Do what you say you will do

Trust others

Recognize and celebrate

Share power

Develop people

Give freedom

Never betray confidence

Speak truth

keep your word.

Be curious

ask questions.

PMA: Positive Mental Attitude

it's why some survive, and others don't.

Positive self-talk

set goals.

Darwin didn't say the strongest survive

he said the most adaptable do.

Think win-win.

"I will not lie, steal, or cheat,

nor tolerate those who do."[18]

Pareto Principle:[19]

80% of effects come from 20% of causes.

Read The Checklist Manifesto.[20]

Understand Crew Resource Management (CRM).

Adopted in totality

it could save lives in the fire service

and improve performance

in other professions.

Understand High Reliability Organization (HRO).[21]

Another game changer.

Understand Red Teaming

Understand Systems Thinking

Think in systems

Challenge the system

TAILBOARD: LEADERSHIP

It's important you understand basic leadership principles. For one, you already are a leader. Everybody is. Whether you know it or not, you already exercise leadership. Leadership is a choice, not a position.

Two, you will work with and for a variety of leaders with various leadership styles during your lifetime. You should know what good leadership looks like, and also what poor leadership looks like.

In sharing my thoughts on leadership, it's important you keep my background in mind. I was a leader in local and state public government agencies. I served as a captain, battalion chief, and division chief on the fire department, and as a program director, director, and academic senator at the university. I'm not sharing leadership ideas from a background where management wields power over fellow human beings to decrease expenses and maximize a profit margin through the labor of others.

There are literally thousands upon thousands of books on leadership. I've read a few dozen of them. I encourage you to do the same. Read a few leadership books and gain an idea of what leadership is about.

The truth is, despite my leadership roles, I consider myself an average leader. I quickly realized leadership develops over a lifetime, not in a day. It takes discipline to become a good leader, and leadership is very challenging work. The books make it sound easy. It is not.

Most importantly, and the real reason I'm sharing leadership principles with you, is that you must know how to lead yourself and your family. As John C. Maxwell states, "Your leadership—for better or worse—always determines your effectiveness and the potential impact you will have."[22]

Before defining leadership, I want to speak about followership. Good followership is as necessary as good leadership. In our culture, premium is placed on being a charismatic, extroverted leader who "gets things done." You know, the one who makes the company and shareholders money. It's assumed by default in this model that followers are docile, passive, obedient simpletons. This is not followership.

Followership is a social relationship between you and your boss. Rather than being a passive passenger along for the ride, good followers engage with their boss and use critical and creative thinking to interact with and share in the leadership process. Don't be afraid to respectfully share ideas that may conflict with your boss's ideas, if you really believe in your ideas. Your boss is looking for people who want to make the organization better. If you never speak up and share, you're not making the organization better.

Learn to be a respectful, active, and engaged follower. Contribute. Your leadership will appreciate it, and you'll become a more effective future leader.

I encourage you to read and study followership, as well as leadership. I learned more about leadership in my studies of followership than I ever did in studying leadership. It's a weird paradox.

Incidentally, if you work for a boss and within an organizational culture where leadership doesn't want to hear from others and has no respect for others' ideas, I encourage you to leave the organization when the timing is right in your life. A closed-minded culture will suck your soul out, eventually. An authoritarian, tyrannical dictator is not a leader. Trust me on this one, make a plan to leave, and quit when the timing is right. When considering a new job, evaluate the leadership in the organization. This is important.

As there are books on leadership, so there are leadership definitions, many of them. Once again, I turn to John C. Maxwell. He defines leadership as "influence, nothing more, nothing less."[23] It's a short definition, but it hits the mark. I like it because it recognizes that leadership can be happening at any level of the organization, and within the family unit and community.

Are you influencing your family? You're a leader.

Leadership is the art of bringing a group of people (employees, family, community) together, willingly, to chase after a vision because they want to, not because they have to. In a formal position of leadership, it's easy to "tell" people to do something. It's much harder to inspire people to want to do something on their own because they believe in it.

If a leader abuses their formal position, pulls rank, too often, they lose credibility and the ability to lead. Just because you can tell somebody to do something because you're the boss doesn't mean you ought to. You should do more modeling and vision-casting than telling. Play the leadership card—"because I told you to"— very, very infrequently, if ever.

Implied in leadership is the ability to formulate and cast a vision that people can see and believe in. Leaders show the way forward, paint a picture of the future, and share their vision in a compelling and believable manner, so much so that followers want to get there on their own without being told.

When John F. Kennedy cast a vision of putting a man on the moon, the scientific community and the American people believed in the vision, and made it happen.

Martin Luther King, Jr. had a dream that one day little Black and white children would play together. Years later, the U.S. elected its first African-American president, Barack H. Obama.

Vision-casting is important in leadership. Where does vision come from? To answer this, I think we need to go to metaphysical foundations and ask: Where does deep vision come from? Don't gloss over the question. I'm not going to answer it for you, but I draw your attention to it. Where does deep vision come from?

When thinking about vision, never forget the people and community. Vision is not about making money. It's about creating quality of life in community. If money follows, excellent.

Leadership is like the learning process, in that we can observe leadership behavior. We only know learning has occurred when we observe a change in behavior. Leadership, like learning, is behavior that can be observed. That's why it's essential to reflect, to debrief, and to loop (observe, orient, decide, act) often. Conduct your own After Action Reviews. Tighten the learning cycle.

We know good leadership when we see it, but what are we seeing?

Leadership is a combined set of skills, performance dimensions, that, when collectively developed, add up and make for good leadership. As each skill is developed, a person begins to look, sound, and act more and more like a leader. Here are the skills that need to be developed and refined if you wish to become a good leader:

- Problem Analysis – ability to seek out relevant data and analyze it; searching for information with purpose; critical evaluation.
- Planning/Organizing – ability to plan, schedule, and control the work of others; skill in resource management; time prioritization.

- Decisiveness – ability to recognize when a decision is needed and act quickly. Slow is smooth. Smooth is fast.
- Leadership – ability to get others involved in problem-solving; guide groups to task completion.
- Interpersonal Skills – ability to perceive needs, resolve conflict, and deal effectively with diversity and emotion.
- Oral Communication – ability to speak clearly and with presence.
- Written Communication – ability to express ideas clearly in writing for varied audiences.
- Situational Awareness – perception of what's going on; balancing details with the big picture; decision-making and follow-up.
- Stress Tolerance – ability to think on your feet under pressure.
- Sensitivity – ability to empathize and meet people where they are.
- Range of Interests – knowledge across topics; staying informed; understanding perspectives.
- Ethics – ability to make tough, right decisions; prioritize principle over profit.

Vision + ethics + courage + reality = leadership.

So, are leaders born or made?

They are made. Through focused effort, through the development of these skills.

Two schools of thought here: one says focus on your strengths and develop them further. The other says work across the board, even on your weaknesses. I believe in both. Use your strengths. But identify weaknesses, and grow those skills too. I was weakest in decisiveness, and I'm glad I worked on it. It helped me in every role I served.

I want to share the concept of referent leadership, or non-positional leadership. Often, it's not the person with the title who's leading, but the one with the influence. Sometimes, I saw firefighters lead more effectively than the captain. Leadership is behavior that can be observed, and influence can come from any level.

Keep this in mind: You don't need a formal title to lead. You can lead from anywhere. Leadership is influence, nothing more, nothing less. Develop your leadership skills. Cast a deep-rooted, metaphysical vision. And then lead.

Lastly, understand that leadership is relational and emotional. Because people have open-loop limbic systems and "speak" to each other on a biochemical level, leaders necessarily set the emotional tone of the family or organization.[24] People look to the leader for guidance. Whether you're a referent leader or a formal one—always set a good tone and a positive emotional climate. DWYSYWD. Do what you say you will do. That's where trust begins.

In closing this brief leadership primer, I quote from The Centurion Principles: Battlefield Lessons for Frontline Leaders by Colonel Jeff O'Leary (Ret.).[25] This is a book you should read:

The Oath of a Centurion

> A battle-hardened legionnaire was promoted to the rank of Centurion based on at least sixteen years of combat service and valor at the point of the spear. He was able to carry ninety pounds of equipment at least twenty miles per day and train under the harshest of conditions. The Centurion was required to equip

himself at his own expense and pay for his own food, clothing, bedding, boots, arms, armor, and dues to the burial club.

He held ultimate sway over the welfare of every man who served in his hundred-man century. The enlistment period was for twenty-five years, after which a cash payment and small plot of land were provided.

To rise to Centurion was considered the highest honor a legionnaire could attain.

A Centurion always led his troops from the front.

———

ACKNOWLEDGMENTS

We never walk alone, do we? Behind this book are a lot of good people who have shaped my life, taught me lessons, and held space for my growth. I owe each of them more than words can express.

My deepest gratitude goes to my wife, Victoria, my anchor. Your patience during my fire department career, our Montana-Tucson commuting years, and your steady presence through every chapter of our story has made all the difference.

To my children, CJ, Carse, Coop, and Grace, thank you for being my greatest teachers, I love you all. Our road trips, your questions about life's meaning, your dreams of cottages on Coronado Island, your companionship at life events, all of it has shaped this book in ways you may never know. I wrote this book with you in my heart.

To my parents, who nurtured my early interest in medicine, gave me Grey's Anatomy for Christmas, and introduced me to faith, thank you. Mom, for dragging me to church by my ears, and Dad, your "Live, Love, and Learn" philosophy lives on in these pages.

To my brother, who has walked through the very gates of hell with me. I've learned as much from you as you have from me.

To the fire service that shaped most of my adult life, thank you for the brotherhood, the lessons, and the kitchen table conversations that formed the backbone of my worldview.

To Bret Tarver, whose fatherhood taught me more than any parenting book ever could.

To JV, whose courage in the face of death taught me what it means to live well, your memory continues to live with me.

To the craftsmen and workers of Montana and Pittsburgh, whose working-class dignity reminds me that knowledge comes through our hands as much as our minds.

To the spiritual guides who've shaped my journey, the Dominican lightning of Dr. O'Brien at Phoenix Community College, the silent welcome of Quaker meeting houses, the grounding practices of Buddhist meditation centers, the Catholic traditions that first shaped my faith, and the Lasallian principles that informed my teaching. To Spirit Rock Meditation Center and UCLA Mindful Awareness Research Center, thank you for tools that healed my fire service wounds.

To the thinkers whose ideas flow through these pages, John Wooden, whose definition of success shapes my understanding; Dr. Michael Ungar and Dr. Ann S. Masten, whose research on resilience informs my understanding of human strength; Oriah Mountain Dreamer, whose invitation to stand in the center of the fire resonates with every firefighter's soul; Thomas Aquinas, who showed us virtue lives in the middle path; and John C. Maxwell, who defined leadership simply as influence.

To the modern prophets who've helped me understand our technological age, Glenn Greenwald, Edward Snowden, and Noam Chomsky, thank you for speaking truth to power.

To my colleagues, and especially students, at Montana State University Billings and San Miguel High School in Tucson, thank you for classroom spaces where I could test these ideas and see them take root in young minds.

To my fifth-grade teacher, Bonnie, who first taught me about grit and living in burned out trees, and to Navy SEALs instructors who later showed me how mental performance shapes physical outcomes.

To Chaplain Ochoa, whose marriage advice literally saved my relationship, and Dr. Lee C. Stuart, who taught me to be a "loyal opponent" instead of a devil's advocate, small shifts in perspective that changed everything.

To my cousin KK in Bozeman, whose insight about celebration helped me understand life's meaning, thank you for that sacred conversation.

To Firefighters Without Borders and our hosts at Kibbutz Yad Mordechai, thank you for showing me what grounded community looks like.

To Zeke, Whitney, Ry, Luu, Abby W., Reyna, and all my students past and present, your young souls have been worth every effort. I hope this book serves you well.

To my early readers, Kendall Taylor, Zeke Holm, Marilyn Pilkey, and Rachel S., thank you for valuable feedback that shaped this final version.

If I've missed anyone, and surely I have missed many, know that the omission lives in my limited words, not my grateful heart. As fire crews say on the fire ground when all crews are accounted for, "We have a PAR; all personnel are present and accounted for."

———

ENDNOTES

INTRODUCTION

1. Bret Tarver was a Phoenix firefighter and friend who died in the line of duty during the Southwest Supermarket fire on March 4, 2001. See the official incident report: Phoenix Fire Department. 'Southwest Supermarket Fire: Phoenix, Arizona, LODD Firefighter Bret Tarver.' March 14, 2001. *Fire Engineering*, www.fireengineering.com/wp-content/uploads/2023/03/phoenix-southwest-supermarket-fire-report.pdf. Accessed 13 May 2025.

1. FOUNDATIONS

1. "First, do no harm." Commonly associated with the Hippocratic Oath, though this exact phrase is a paraphrase and not present in the original Greek text.
2. "All men are created equal." Declaration of Independence, 1776.
3. "To thine own self be true." Shakespeare, William. Hamlet, Act I, Scene III.
4. "Between stimulus and response, there is a gap..." Often attributed to Viktor E. Frankl. Paraphrased from Man's Search for Meaning.
5. "Virtue is the means, the middle..." Paraphrased from Aristotle. Nicomachean Ethics. Public domain.
6. "Honesty is the best policy." Commonly attributed to Benjamin Franklin; widely used proverb.
7. "Form follows function." Sullivan, Louis H. Essay: "The Tall Office Building Artistically Considered," Lippincott's Magazine, March 1896.
8. "Develop a seventh generation mindset." Based on Indigenous (Haudenosaunee) philosophy of environmental and generational responsibility.
9. "All is grace." Widely used phrase in Christian theology. Popularized in modern times by Brennan Manning in All Is Grace.
10. "The deed is all." Echoes literary and philosophical themes; similar in tone to Shakespeare's King Lear ("Ripeness is all").

2. DAD'S LIST

1. The concept of living in your "3-foot world" is commonly associated with military and first responder training, particularly Navy SEAL training. It refers to focusing only on what's immediately in front of you rather than becoming overwhelmed by the larger situation.

2. The "1% better each day" concept has been popularized in recent performance psychology and personal development literature, notably in James Clear's Atomic Habits.
3. "CareerCast's 2015 Most Stressful Jobs Report." CareerCast, 2015.
4. "Most Stressful Jobs of 2015." Forbes, 2015.
5. "Statistics." National Center for PTSD, U.S. Department of Veterans Affairs.
6. Berninger, A., et al. "Trends of probable post-traumatic stress disorder in New York City after the September 11 terrorist attacks." American Journal of Epidemiology, 2010.
7. Bernabé, M., & Botia, J. M. "PTSD and Coping Among Career Professional Firefighters." Journal of Occupational Health Psychology, 2016.
8. Mindfulness-Based Mind Fitness Training (MMFT) was developed by Elizabeth Stanley, PhD, for high-stress operational environments.
9. "Mindful Awareness Practices (MAPs) I." UCLA Mindful Awareness Research Center, semel.ucla.edu.

3. LIFE

1. Variation of "Better is he that giveth." Christian proverb with roots in Biblical teachings.
2. Line commonly attributed to various sources in popular culture.
3. Folklore saying found in several cultures.
4. Common educational and life philosophy mantras. These sayings were frequently quoted by Colin McCoy, the author's father, whose wisdom continues to inspire generations of his family.
5. Adaptation of Woody Allen's quote, "Eighty percent of success is showing up."
6. "Garbage in, garbage out" (GIGO). Computing principle from CJ McCoy, who learned this from his high school math teacher, Mr. Linton. Originated in late 1950s computer programming, emphasizing that flawed input produces flawed output.
7. "Walk softly and carry a big stick." Adapted from President Theodore Roosevelt's foreign policy maxim "Speak softly and carry a big stick; you will go far," and reinforced through personal wisdom shared by Colin McCoy (author's father).
8. Common phrase in recovery and 12-step programs. This saying was frequently quoted by Kathy Cathey, the author's mother, whose wisdom continues to inspire generations of his family.
9. Covey, Stephen R. The 7 Habits of Highly Effective People. Free Press, 1989.
10. Churchill, Winston. Speech at Harrow School, October 29, 1941.
11. Adaptation of quote often attributed to John A. Shedd, "A ship in harbor is safe, but that is not what ships are built for."
12. Common career/life coaching questions.
13. Matthew 6:34, from Jesus' Sermon on the Mount.
14. Paraphrase of a saying attributed to Paulo Coelho.

15. Street/prison slang that became a popular phrase in broader culture.
16. "Measure twice, cut once." Traditional carpentry wisdom. Public domain.
17. Thoreau, Henry David. Walden. 1854.
18. Reference to popular dance music/culture.
19. Wholehearted School Counseling is a resource for educational professionals.
20. Often attributed to Edmund Burke, though the exact quote is disputed.
21. "The pen is mightier than the sword." Edward Bulwer-Lytton, *Richelieu; Or the Conspiracy*, 1839. Public domain.
22. Kipling, Rudyard. The Jungle Book. 1894.
23. Nietzsche, Friedrich. Twilight of the Idols. 1888.
24. Adaptation of Lao Tzu's "A journey of a thousand miles begins with a single step."
25. Shackleton, Ernest. Apocryphal advertisement for Antarctic expedition crew.
26. Military principle, particularly emphasized in U.S. armed forces.
27. Common phrase in firefighting, signifying solidarity.
28. Pascal, Blaise. Pensées. 1670.
29. Adaptation of quote often attributed to Mark Twain, "History doesn't repeat itself, but it often rhymes."
30. "Take the long view seven generations." Traditional Native American wisdom, particularly associated with Haudenosaunee (Iroquois) philosophy of considering the impact of decisions on seven generations into the future. Public domain.
31. Common counterculture phrase, censored here.

4. RELATIONSHIPS

1. "Happy is the man who has his quiver full of children" is from Psalm 127:5.
2. "Watch how boys treat their mothers, it tells you how they might treat their future wife." Commonly attributed to William Summerville, though source unverified. Widely circulated parenting wisdom.
3. The concept of marriage as a symbol of Christ and the Church comes from Ephesians 5:22-33.
4. This advice appears is from a personal conversation with a fire department chaplain.
5. This "In our home" list is a popular home decor phrase/concept, variations of which appear in many places.
6. Mark 6:7.
7. "If you go, we go" is a firefighting motto expressing commitment to never leave anyone behind.

5. FAITH & WISDOM

1. Paraphrase of Christian community concept, particularly from Matthew 18:20.
2. "Every single one has that of which is God within them." Foundational Quaker belief in the "Inner Light" or "Light of Christ" within all people. Traditional Quaker theology.
3. Luke 1:38, Mary's response to the angel Gabriel.
4. Luke 2:52, describing Jesus' development.
5. James 1:27.
6. Concept from James 1:19-26 and Proverbs 21:23.
7. Ephesians 2:8.
8. 1 Thessalonians 4:11.
9. Joshua 1:9.
10. Joshua 24:15.
11. The Serenity Prayer, attributed to Reinhold Niebuhr.
12. C.T. Studd, missionary to China, India, and Africa.
13. Micah 6:8.
14. Jeremiah 29:11.
15. Matthew 7:1, from Jesus' Sermon on the Mount.
16. Matthew 7:3— from Jesus' Sermon on the Mount.
17. Mark 12:30-31.
18. Exodus 20:3-17.
19. John 3:16.
20. The Hail Mary prayer, based on Luke 1:28, 42.
21. The Lord's Prayer from Matthew 6:9-13.
22. From Catholic catechism and Thomas Aquinas' teachings.
23. Various passages from Ecclesiastes combined with Matthew 5:41.
24. Psalm 23.
25. Isaiah 40:31.
26. 2 Samuel 23:20.
27. Luke 10:25-37.
28. Foundational Buddhist teaching.
29. The Five Pillars of Islam are considered the foundation of Muslim life, as established in the Quran and through the teachings of Prophet Muhammad. See "The Pillars of Islam and Iman," in Sahih Al-Bukhari, translated by Muhammad Muhsin Khan, Vol. 1, Book 2, Hadith 7-8.
30. Quote attributed to Sherpa wisdom.
31. Anatoli Boukreev, Himalayan mountain climber.
32. Hindu greeting and concept.
33. John 11:35.
34. Matthew 6:26, 28, from Jesus' Sermon on the Mount.
35. Adaptation of a quote often attributed to various sources.
36. The Jesus Prayer from Eastern Orthodox tradition.

37. Romans 8:19.
38. William Blake, "Auguries of Innocence."
39. Buddhist mantra of compassion.
40. "There is no God but God" (La ilaha illa Allah) is the first part of the Shahada, the Islamic declaration of faith. This fundamental testimony appears throughout the Quran, including Surah 3:18 and Surah 47:19. See Nasr, Seyyed Hossein. "The Heart of Islam: Enduring Values for Humanity." Harper-One, 2004, p. 3.
41. Brahmanism: "This is the sum of Dharma: Do naught unto others which would cause you pain if done to you." *Mahabharata*, 5:1517.
42. Buddhism: "Hurt not others in ways that you yourself would find hurtful." *Udana-Varga*, 5:18.
43. Christianity: "So in everything, do to others what you would have them do to you, for this sums up the Law and the Prophets." *The Holy Bible*, New International Version, Matthew 7:12.
44. Confucianism: "Do not do to others what you do not want them to do to you." *The Doctrine of the Mean*.
45. Hinduism: "This is the sum of duty: do not do to others what would cause pain if done to you." *Mahabharata*, 5:1517.
46. "The Islamic formulation of the Golden Rule is expressed in a hadith (recorded saying of Prophet Muhammad): 'None of you truly believes until he loves for his brother what he loves for himself.' This appears in the two most authoritative hadith collections, Sahih Bukhari and Sahih Muslim, and is included as the thirteenth hadith in Imam Nawawi's collection of Forty Hadith, a widely studied compilation in Islamic tradition. Similar expressions of this principle appear in other hadith, including 'Whoever wishes to be delivered from the fire and to enter Paradise should treat the people as he wishes to be treated.'"
47. The religion of the Incas: "Do not to another what you would not yourself experience." Manco Capoc, founder of the empire of Peru.
48. Judaism: "...thou shalt love thy neighbor as thyself." *The Holy Bible*, King James Version, Leviticus 19:18.
49. Native American Spirituality: "Respect for all life is the foundation." *The Great Law of Peace*.

6. RESILIENCE

1. Nichols, Wallace J. Blue Mind: The Surprising Science That Shows How Being Near, In, On, or Under Water Can Make You Happier, Healthier, More Connected, and Better at What You Do. Little, Brown and Company, 2014.
2. Japanese proverb: "Fall down seven times, get up eight." Traditional Japanese saying. Public domain.
3. Masten, Ann S. Ordinary Magic: Resilience in Development. Guilford Press, 2014.

4. Ungar, Michael. "About Resilience." Resilience Research Centre, https://resilienceresearch.org/about-resilience/. Accessed April 2025.

5. Across resilience literature, five core typologies consistently appear: persistence, resistance, recovery, adaptation, and transformation. These are used across fields from developmental psychology to systems ecology to describe how individuals and systems respond to adversity and change.

6. Sapolsky, Robert M. Why Zebras Don't Get Ulcers. 3rd ed., Holt Paperbacks, 2004.

7. Ungar, Michael. R2 Resilience Expert Training Course. Resilience Research Centre, 2025, https://resilienceresearch.org/expert-training/.

8. van der Kolk, Bessel A. The Body Keeps the Score: Brain, Mind, and Body in the Healing of Trauma. Penguin Books, 2014.

9. Hebb, Donald O. The Organization of Behavior: A Neuropsychological Theory. Wiley, 1949.

10. Always consult your doctor or a qualified medical professional before starting or changing any supplement routine. This book does not offer medical advice.

11. The distinction between rugged and resourced protective factors comes from Dr. Michael Ungar's Resilience R2 Expert Resilience Training, developed by the Resilience Research Centre. For more, see: Ungar, Michael. "About Resilience." Resilience Research Centre, https://resilienceresearch.org/about-resilience/. Accessed April 2025.

12. "Sisu." Finnish concept meaning extraordinary determination and resoluteness in the face of extreme adversity. Variously translated as stoic determination, tenacity of purpose, grit, bravery, resilience, and hardiness. Traditional Finnish cultural philosophy.

13. Duckworth, Angela. Grit: The Power of Passion and Perseverance. Scribner, 2016.

14. Duckworth, Angela. "Grit: The Power of Passion and Perseverance." TED Talks, Apr. 2013, www.ted.com/talks/angela_lee_duckworth_grit_the_power_of_passion_and_perseverance.

15. Byron, Chris. Personal presentation at the Pathways to Resilience III: Beyond Nature vs. Nurture Conference, Halifax, Nova Scotia, Oct. 2015.

7. MINIMALISM

1. Excerpted from Endure: A Memoir of Grief, Resilience, and Love by Kelly McCoy. Ei²Collective, 2024.

2. Harnden, Philip. Journeys of Simplicity: Traveling Light with Thomas Merton, Basho, Edward Abbey, Annie Dillard, and Others. Skylight Paths Publishing, 2003.

3. Couturier, Andy. The Abundance of Less: Lessons in Simple Living from Rural Japan. North Atlantic Books, 2017.

4. VandenBroeck, Goldian. Less Is More: An Anthology of Ancient and Modern Voices Raised in Praise of Simplicity. Inner Traditions, 2000.

5. "Use it up, wear it out, make it do, or do without." Traditional American proverb, commonly associated with the Great Depression and WWII-era frugality. Public domain.

6. Harnden, Philip. *Journeys of Simplicity: Traveling Light with Thomas Merton, Basho, Edward Abbey, Annie Dillard, and Others.* Skylight Paths Publishing, 2003.

7. "Less is more." Popularized by architect Ludwig Mies van der Rohe, mid-20th century. Public domain.

8. Palahniuk, Chuck. *Fight Club.* W.W. Norton & Company, 1996.

9. "Simplify. Simplify. Simplify." Paraphrased from Henry David Thoreau, *Walden,* 1854. Public domain.

10. *20 Liter Life.* Accessed 25 Apr. 2025, http://20literlife.com/

8. POETRY

1. "Surfing the Wave." Found on the wall of the Yellow Book Road Bookstore, San Diego, circa 2005. Author unknown. Included here with appreciation for its anonymous beauty and inspiration.

2. "Irish Blessing." Traditional. Public domain. Commonly cited as: "May the road rise up to meet you..."

3. Donne, John. "For Whom the Bell Tolls." *Devotions upon Emergent Occasions,* 1624. Public domain.

4. Roosevelt, Theodore. "Citizenship in a Republic." Speech delivered at the Sorbonne, Paris, 23 April 1910. Public domain.

5. Issa. "The Puppy Asleep." Traditional haiku, circa early 19th century. Translation in public domain.

6. Buson. "In the Winter River." Traditional haiku, 18th century. Translation in public domain.

7. Buson. "My Bones." Traditional haiku, 18th century. Translation in public domain.

8. Frost, Robert. "The Road Not Taken." *Mountain Interval,* Henry Holt and Co., 1916. Public domain.

9. Kipling, Rudyard. "If—." *Rewards and Fairies,* Macmillan, 1910. Public domain.

10. Henley, William Ernest. "Invictus." 1875. Public domain.

11. "The Tiger and the Strawberry" is a traditional Zen parable passed down through oral teachings and storytelling. Source unknown. Public domain.

12. Dreamer, Oriah Mountain. *The Invitation.* HarperOne, 1999. Excerpted with respect and gratitude to Oriah Mountain Dreamer. More at www.oriahmountaindreamer.com.

9. SCREENS & TECHNOLOGY

1. Citizenfour. Directed by Laura Poitras, performances by Edward Snowden, Glenn Greenwald, and William Binney, Praxis Films, 2014.
2. Shlain, Tiffany. 24/6: The Power of Unplugging One Day a Week. Gallery Books, 2019.
3. Orlowski, Jeff, director. The Social Dilemma. Netflix, 2020.
4. Winner, Langdon. The Whale and the Reactor: A Search for Limits in an Age of High Technology. University of Chicago Press, 1986.
5. Haidt, Jonathan. The Anxious Generation: How the Great Rewiring of Childhood Is Causing an Epidemic of Mental Illness. Penguin Press, 2024.
6. Young, James. Infinity. Better Company Records, 2023.
7. Manufacturing Consent: Noam Chomsky and the Media. Directed by Mark Achbar and Peter Wintonick, performances by Noam Chomsky and Edward S. Herman, Necessary Illusions and Zeitgeist Films, 1992.

10. ECONOMIC & POLITICS

1. "Some people are so poor, all they have is money." Commonly attributed to Patrick Meagher and Bob Marley, though the original source remains uncertain.
2. "Compound interest is the eighth wonder of the world." Commonly attributed to Albert Einstein, though no verified source exists. Public domain quotation.
3. Kibbe, Matt. Don't Hurt People and Don't Take Their Stuff: A Libertarian Manifesto. HarperCollins, 2014.
4. Thoreau, Henry David. Civil Disobedience and Other Essays. Dover Publications, 1993.
5. The Vandals. "Anarchy Burger (Hold the Government)." Peace Thru Vandalism, Epitaph Records, 1982.
6. Butler, Smedley D., General, United States Marine Corps, War Is a Racket. Round Table Press, 1935.
7. "There are two ways to be rich—by acquiring much or desiring little." Attributed to Jackie F. Collar. Source unverified; widely circulated aphorism.
8. The concept of libertarian socialism combines personal freedom with community responsibility, emphasizing both individual autonomy and collective solidarity. Notable thinkers in this tradition include Noam Chomsky and Murray Bookchin. For an introduction to these ideas, see Chomsky, Noam. 'On Anarchism.' New Press, 2013, and Bookchin, Murray. 'The Next Revolution: Popular Assemblies and the Promise of Direct Democracy.' Verso, 2015. This political philosophy advocates for a balance between liberty and equality without the authoritarian aspects of state socialism or the potential inequalities of unrestrained capitalism.

9. Achbar, Mark, and Peter Wintonick, directors. Manufacturing Consent: Noam Chomsky and the Media. Necessary Illusions, 1992.

11. WORK

1. "Early to bed and early to rise makes a man healthy, wealthy, and wise." Commonly attributed to Benjamin Franklin, Poor Richard's Almanack, 1735. Public domain.
2. Wooden, John. Wooden: A Lifetime of Observations and Reflections On and Off the Court. McGraw-Hill, 1997.
3. "Where the needs of the world and your passions intersect, there lies your vocation." Commonly paraphrased from Aristotle. Original source unverified; widely attributed.
4. Myers, Isabel Briggs, and Peter B. Myers. Gifts Differing: Understanding Personality Type. Nicholas Brealey Publishing, 1995.
5. Winkler, Irwin, director. Life as a House. Performances by Kevin Kline, Kristin Scott Thomas, and Hayden Christensen, New Line Cinema, 2001.

12. SAFETY

1. "To err is human." Alexander Pope, An Essay on Criticism, 1711. Public domain.
2. Most fatalities on Mount Everest occur during descent. See: Huey, Raymond B., and Michael E. Salisbury. "Success and Death on Mount Everest: 1921–2006." British Medical Journal, vol. 337, 2008, doi:10.1136/bmj.a2654.
3. "Three to go, one no-go" is a safety principle widely used in air medical transport, emphasizing unanimous crew consent for flight decisions.
4. Mark 6:7.

13. LEARNING

1. Paraphrased from Socratic wisdom and often quoted by Colin McCoy (author's father).
2. McCoy, Colin. Personal reflection. Quoted with love and admiration by his son.
3. McCoy, Colin. Personal reflection.
4. Covey, Stephen R. The 7 Habits of Highly Effective People. Free Press, 1989.
5. "I hear and I forget, I see and I remember, I do and I understand." Traditional Chinese proverb. Public domain.
6. Wilbur, Laura F. "Writing is the closest thing we have to real magic." Widely attributed; source unverified.
7. "Give a man a fish..." Traditional proverb. Public domain.
8. Breen, Mike. Building a Discipling Culture: How to Release a Missional Movement by Discipling People Like Jesus Did. 3DM Publishing, 2011. This "see

one, do one, teach one" model of progressive learning is widely used in both discipleship and vocational training.

9. Bernays, Edward. *Propaganda*. Ig Publishing, 2005. Originally published 1928.
10. These reflections were written during my time as a Division Chief of Training (2009–2014). I wrote most of them while actively developing as a Chief Training Officer—a credential I've held through the Center for Public Safety Excellence since 2014. I hold a Master's in Education (M.Ed.) and have taught Fire Science at Montana State University Billings. Later, I served as Director for Fire Training at The University of Kansas. This writing reflects hard-won lessons, field-tested ideas, and the pursuit of what Oliver Wendell Holmes called "the simplicity on the far side of complexity."

14. LEADERSHIP

1. Boyd, John. *The Essence of Winning and Losing*. Briefing, 1995.
2. "APIE: Analyze, Plan, Implement, Evaluate." Standard framework in hazardous materials and emergency response training. Public domain.
3. "After Action Review (AAR)." National Wildfire Coordinating Group (NWCG), U.S. Department of the Interior, www.nwcg.gov/term/after-action-review. Accessed April 2025.
4. Maxwell, John C. *The 21 Irrefutable Laws of Leadership*. Thomas Nelson, 2007.
5. Goleman, Daniel, Richard Boyatzis, and Annie McKee. *Primal Leadership: Unleashing the Power of Emotional Intelligence*. Harvard Business Review Press, 2002.
6. Kouzes, James M., and Barry Z. Posner. *The Leadership Challenge: How to Make Extraordinary Things Happen in Organizations*. Jossey-Bass, 1987.
7. "Your thoughts become your words..." is commonly attributed to Frank Outlaw, former president of Bi-Lo Stores, and has been widely circulated in various forms since the 1970s. Original phrasing varies; included here for its enduring insight.
8. Doran, George T. "There's a S.M.A.R.T. Way to Write Management's Goals and Objectives." *Management Review*, vol. 70, no. 11, 1981, pp. 35–36.
9. Holmes, Oliver Wendell. Quoted in various sources. Original phrasing attributed to public speeches; widely paraphrased and in public domain.
10. Sinek, Simon. *Leaders Eat Last: Why Some Teams Pull Together and Others Don't*. Portfolio, 2014.
11. *The Holy Bible*, New King James Version. Thomas Nelson, 1982. Proverbs 29:18.
12. "Three improves / three sustains" AAR format introduced during an O2X Human Performance workshop, Montana, 2019. Field-based adaptation shared by instructors with backgrounds in U.S. Navy Special Operations. Included here from the author's direct experience.

13. The concept of being a "loyal opponent" was introduced to the author by Dr. Lee C. Stuart during a Certified Public Management (CPM) training program at the University of Kansas in 2023. Dr. Stuart brings experience across journalism, corporate leadership, and executive coaching, and holds a Doctorate in Business Administration/Leadership Studies from Capella University.

14. Grossman, Dave. On Combat: The Psychology and Physiology of Deadly Conflict in War and in Peace. Warrior Science Publications, 2004.

15. Heraclitus. Quoted in various military and leadership contexts. Original Greek text lost; paraphrased in modern translations. Public domain.

16. Collins, Jim, and Jerry I. Porras. Built to Last: Successful Habits of Visionary Companies. HarperBusiness, 1994.

17. John C. Maxwell. Leadership development questions. Contemporary leadership author and speaker.

18. "Cadet Honor Code." United States Military Academy at West Point. www.westpoint.edu. Accessed April 2025.

19. Pareto, Vilfredo. Cours d'économie politique. 1896. Principle now known as the 80/20 Rule.

20. Gawande, Atul. The Checklist Manifesto: How to Get Things Right. Metropolitan Books, 2009.

21. Weick, Karl E., and Kathleen M. Sutcliffe. Managing the Unexpected: Resilient Performance in an Age of Uncertainty. 3rd ed., Wiley, 2015.

22. Maxwell, John C. The 21 Irrefutable Laws of Leadership: Follow Them and People Will Follow You. Thomas Nelson, 2007.

23. Maxwell, John C. The 21 Irrefutable Laws of Leadership: Follow Them and People Will Follow You. Thomas Nelson, 2007.

24. Goleman, Daniel, Richard Boyatzis, and Annie McKee. Primal Leadership: Unleashing the Power of Emotional Intelligence. Harvard Business Review Press, 2002.

25. O'Leary, Jeff. The Centurion Principles: Battlefield Lessons for Frontline Leaders. Thomas Nelson, 2003.

RESOURCES

Resources

The following resources have shaped the ideas in this book and are offered for those who wish to explore these topics more deeply. Each section corresponds to a chapter and includes books, articles, films, and online materials that complement the themes discussed.

CHAPTER 1: FOUNDATIONS

Books and Texts

- Aristotle. Nicomachean Ethics.
- Frankl, Viktor E. Man's Search for Meaning.
- George, Jean Craighead. My Side of the Mountain.
- Gray, Henry. Grey's Anatomy.
- Manning, Brennan. All Is Grace.
- Shakespeare, William. Hamlet.

Documents and Philosophy

- The Declaration of Independence
- The Hippocratic Oath
- Works on Haudenosaunee (Iroquois) seventh generation philosophy

CHAPTER 2: DAD'S LIST

Mindfulness and Resilience

- Mindful Awareness Practices I through the UCLA Mindful Awareness Research Center: semel.ucla.edu/marc
- Spirit Rock: An Insight Meditation Center: spiritrock.org
- Stanley, Elizabeth A. Widen the Window: Training Your Brain and Body to Thrive During Stress and Recover from Trauma.

Personal Development

- Clear, James. Atomic Habits: An Easy & Proven Way to Build Good Habits & Break Bad Ones.
- Owen, Mark and Kevin Maurer. No Easy Day: The Firsthand Account of the Mission That Killed Osama Bin Laden.

Community and Alternative Living

- Spiro, Melford. Kibbutz: Venture in Utopia. 1956.

CHAPTER 3: LIFE

Books

- Aurelius, Marcus. Meditations.

- Bruder, Jessica. Nomadland: Surviving America in the Twenty-First Century.
- Buettner, Dan. The Blue Zones: Lessons for Living Longer From the People Who've Lived the Longest.
- Covey, Stephen R. The 7 Habits of Highly Effective People.
- Esolen, Anthony. No Apologies: Why Civilization Depends Upon the Strength of Men.
- Hamsun, Knut. Growth of the Soil.
- Hemingway, Ernest. The Old Man and the Sea.
- Kipling, Rudyard. The Jungle Book.
- Manning, Richard. A Good House: Building a Life on the Land.
- Sundeen, Mark. The Unsettlers: In Search of the Good Life in Today's America.

Films

- On Golden Pond. Directed by Mark Rydell, 1981.

Online Resources

- "My Grandma's Rules for Happiness." Mamalode: mamalode.com/story/mamas-list/my-grandmas-rules-for-happiness
- "What I've Learned from Life and Travel." BootsnAll: bootsnall.com/articles/what-ive-learned-from-life-and-travel.html
- Wholehearted School Counseling: wholeheartedschool-counseling.com

CHAPTER 4: RELATIONSHIPS

Books

- Bonhoeffer, Dietrich. Life Together: The Classic Exploration of Christian Community.
- Brown, Daniel James. The Boys in the Boat: Nine Americans and Their Epic Quest for Gold at the 1936 Berlin Olympics.
- Chapman, Gary. The Five Love Languages.
- Eggers, Dave. A Heartbreaking Work of Staggering Genius.
- Junger, Sebastian. Tribe: On Homecoming and Belonging.
- Kerouac, Jack. On the Road.
- McCarthy, Cormac. The Road.
- Potts, Rolf. Vagabonding: An Uncommon Guide to the Art of Long-Term World Travel.

Travel

- "The Ultimate Pacific Coast Highway itinerary, from San Francisco to Santa Monica." National Geographic: nationalgeographic.com/travel/article/pacific-coast-highway-california-itinerary

CHAPTER 5: FAITH & WISDOM

Books

- Buddhist texts on the Five Precepts and Eightfold Path
- Dalai Lama XIV. The Art of Happiness.
- Drane, James F. Becoming a Good Doctor: The Place of Virtue and Character in Medical Ethics.

- Endo, Shusaku. Silence.
- Escobar, Kathy. Faith Shift: Finding Your Way Forward When Everything You Believe is Coming Apart.
- Manning, Brennan. The Ragamuffin Gospel.
- Merton, Thomas. Conjectures of a Guilty Bystander.
- Merton, Thomas. The Seven Storey Mountain.
- Pirsig, Robert. Zen and the Art of Motorcycle Maintenance: An Inquiry Into Values.
- Platt, David. Radical: Taking Back Your Faith from the American Dream.
- Reps, Paul and Nyogen Senzaki. Zen Flesh, Zen Bones: A Collection of Zen and Pre-Zen Writing.
- Swoboda, A.J. After Doubt: How to Question Your Faith without Losing It.
- The Book of Ecclesiastes
- The Holy Quran
- The Pentateuch and Four Gospels
- Wilson, Frank E. Faith and Practice.
- Wilson, Hersch. Firefighter Zen: A Field Guide to Thriving in Tough Times.

Spirituality and Ethics

- "Five Core Lasallian Principles." Christian Brothers University: cbu.edu/about/lasallian-tradition/five-core-lasallian-principles
- "The Human Virtues-Catechism." The Holy See: vatican.va/content/catechism/en/part_three/section_one/chapter_one/article_7/i_the_human_virtues.html

CHAPTER 6: RESILIENCE

Books

- Divine, Mark. Unbeatable Mind: Forge Resiliency and Mental Toughness to Succeed at an Elite Level.
- Duckworth, Angela. Grit: The Power of Passion and Perseverance.
- Dweck, Carol S. Mindset: The New Psychology of Success.
- Masten, Ann S. Ordinary Magic: Resilience in Development.
- Nichols, Wallace J. Blue Mind: The Surprising Science That Shows How Being Near, In, On, or Under Water Can Make You Happier, Healthier, More Connected, and Better at What You Do.
- Sapolsky, Robert M. Why Zebras Don't Get Ulcers.
- Shanahan, Catherine. Deep Nutrition: Why Your Genes Need Traditional Food.
- Ungar, Michael. Change Your World: The Science of Resilience and the True Path to Success.
- van der Kolk, Bessel. The Body Keeps the Score: Brain, Mind, and Body in the Healing of Trauma.

Research

- Resilience Research Centre: resilienceresearch.org

CHAPTER 7: MINIMALISM

Books

- Cain, Susan. Quiet: The Power of Introverts in a World That Can't Stop Talking.

- Couturier, Andy. The Abundance of Less: Lessons in Simple Living from Rural Japan.
- Harnden, Philip. Journeys of Simplicity: Traveling Light with Thomas Merton, Basho, Edward Abbey, Annie Dillard, and Others.
- Kagge, Erling. Silence: In the Age of Noise.
- Millburn, Joshua Fields. Essential: Essays by The Minimalists.
- Sasaki, Fumio. Goodbye Things: The New Japanese Minimalism.
- Thoreau, Henry David. Walden.
- VandenBroeck, Goldian. Less Is More: An Anthology of Ancient and Modern Voices Raised in Praise of Simplicity.

Digital Resources

- The 20 Liter Life blog: 20literlife.com

Gear

- Ex Officio Men's Give-N-Go® 2.0 Boxer: exofficio.com/underwear/men/boxers/mens-give-n-go-2.0-boxer
- Osprey FarPoint® 40 Travel Pack
- Smartwool Everyday Lifestyle Houndstooth Ankle Socks

CHAPTER 8: POETRY

Books

- Bly, Robert, James Hillman, et al. The Rag and Bone Shop of the Heart: A Poetry Anthology.
- Dreamer, Oriah Mountain. The Invitation.

- Loder, Ted. Guerrillas of Grace: Prayers for the Battle.
- Maclean, Norman. A River Runs Through It.
- Saenz, Benjamin Alire. The Book of What Remains.
- Smythe, Matt. Revision of a Man.
- Stroud, Joseph. Below Cold Mountain.
- Washington, Peter, editor. Haiku. Everyman's Library Pocket Poets Series.

CHAPTER 9: SCREENS & TECHNOLOGY

Films and Documentaries

- Citizenfour. Directed by Laura Poitras, 2014.
- Manufacturing Consent: Noam Chomsky and the Media. Directed by Mark Achbar and Peter Wintonick, 1992.
- The Social Dilemma. Directed by Jeff Orlowski, 2020.

Books

- Brunton, Finn. Obfuscation: A User's Guide for Privacy and Protest.
- Bruder, Jessica. Snowden's Box: Trust in the Age of Surveillance.
- Haidt, Jonathan. The Anxious Generation: How the Great Rewiring of Childhood Is Causing an Epidemic of Mental Illness.
- Harding, Luke. The Snowden Files: The Inside Story of the World's Most Wanted Man.
- Shlain, Tiffany. 24/6: The Power of Unplugging One Day a Week.
- Snowden, Edward. Permanent Record.
- Winner, Langdon. The Whale and the Reactor: A Search for Limits in an Age of High Technology.

CHAPTER 10: ECONOMICS & POLITICS

Books

- Butler, Smedley D. War Is a Racket.
- Chomsky, Noam and Edward S. Herman. Manufacturing Consent: The Political Economy of the Mass Media.
- Dominguez, Joe. Your Money or Your Life.
- Kibbe, Matt. Don't Hurt People and Don't Take Their Stuff: A Libertarian Manifesto.
- Lakey, George. Viking Economics: How the Scandinavians Got It Right- and How We Can, Too.
- Legutko, Ryszard. The Cunning of Freedom: Saving the Self in an Age of False Idols.
- Marx, Karl. The Communist Manifesto.
- Mitchell, Joshua. America Awakening: Identity Politics and Other Afflictions of Our Time.
- Moller, Dan. Governing Least: A New England Libertarianism.
- Schumacher, E.F. Small is Beautiful: Economics as if People Mattered.
- Thoreau, Henry David. Civil Disobedience and Other Essays.

Articles

- "What I Told the Students of Princeton." The Truth Fairy: thetruthfairy.info/p/what-i-told-the-students-of-princeton

CHAPTER 11: WORK

Books

- Biese, Ingrid. Men Do It Too: Opting Out and In.
- Brown, Ryan C. Pittsburgh and the Great Steel Strike of 1919.
- Crawford, Matthew B. Shop Class as Soul Craft: An Inquiry into the Value of Work.
- Gorges, Eric. A Craftsman's Legacy: Why Working with Our Hands Gives Us Meaning.
- Kawasaki, Guy. The Art of the Start: The Time-Tested, Battle-Hardened Guide for Anyone Starting Anything.
- Lind, Diana. Brave New Home: Our Future in Smarter, Simpler, Happier Housing.

Films

- Life as a House. Directed by Irwin Winkler, 2001.

Blogs

- Early Retirement Extreme: earlyretirementextreme.com
- The Opting Out Blog: theoptingoutblog.com

CHAPTER 12: SAFETY

Books

- Geiger, John. The Third Man Factor: The Secret To Survival In Extreme Environments.
- Gonzales, Laurence. Deep Survival: Who Lives, Who Dies, and Why.

- Harris, Alex. Do Hard Things: A Teenage Rebellion Against Low Expectations.
- Krakauer, Jon. Into Thin Air: A Personal Account of the Mt. Everest Disaster.

Articles

- "How Safetyism Killed Playtime." UnHerd: unherd.com/2024/01/how-safetyism-killed-playtime
- "Recess Without Rules." The Atlantic: theatlantic.com/education/archive/2014/01/recess-without-rules/283382

Training and Frameworks

- "Crew Resource Management is a Team Approach to Success." TCI Magazine: tcimag.tcia.org/business-strategy/crew-resource-management-is-a-team-approach-to-success
- "The Tao of Boyd: How to Master the OODA Loop." The Art of Manliness: artofmanliness.com/character/behavior/ooda-loop

CHAPTER 13: LEARNING

Books

- Berger, Ron, Howard Gardner, and Deborah Meier. An Ethic of Excellence: Building a Culture of Craftsmanship with Students.
- Bernays, Edward. Propaganda.
- Breen, Mike. Building a Discipling Culture: How to Release a Missional Movement by Discipling People Like Jesus Did.

- Covey, Stephen R. The 7 Habits of Highly Effective People.

Educational Resources

- After Action Reviews (National Wildfire Coordinating Group): nwcg.gov/wfldp/toolbox/aars
- High Impact Practices (The University of Arizona): hip.ge.arizona.edu/what-are-hips-and-why-use-them

CHAPTER 14: LEADERSHIP

Books

- Chouinard, Yvon. Let My People Go Surfing: The Education of a Reluctant Businessman.
- Gawande, Atul. The Checklist Manifesto: How to Get Things Right.
- Glick-Smith, Judith. Flow-based Leadership: What the Best Firefighters can Teach you about Leadership and Making Hard Decisions.
- Goleman, Daniel, Richard Boyatzis, and Annie McKee. Primal Leadership: Unleashing the Power of Emotional Intelligence.
- Maxwell, John C. The 21 Irrefutable Laws of Leadership: Follow Them and People Will Follow You.
- Meadows, Donella H. Thinking in Systems: A Primer.
- O'Leary, Jeff. The Centurion Principles: Battlefield Lessons for Frontline Leaders.
- Pascale, Richard Tanner. The Art of Japanese Management.
- Sinek, Simon. Leaders Eat Last: Why Some Teams Pull Together and Others Don't.

- Weick, Karl E. and Kathleen M. Sutcliffe. Managing the Unexpected: Resilient Performance in an Age of Uncertainty.
- Wooden, John. Wooden: A Lifetime of Observations and Reflections On and Off the Court.

Articles

- "Followership: Great Skill for Leadership." Ohio State University Fisher College of Business: fisher.osu.edu/blogs/leadreadtoday/followership-great-skill-leadership
- "Followership: It's Personal, Too." Harvard Business Review: hbr.org/2001/12/followership-its-personal-too
- "In Praise of Followers." Harvard Business Review: hbr.org/1988/11/in-praise-of-followers

———

ABOUT THE AUTHOR

Kelly is a husband, father, dog dad, and writer who believes in living a life of presence, grit, and integrity. His writing blends the steady hands of a fire officer, the open heart of a father, and the long view of a philosopher.

A former division chief with 25 years in the fire service, Kelly later transitioned to higher education, serving as a faculty member, mentor, and academic senator. He holds degrees in liberal studies and education, and completed graduate work in philosophy and theology.

Kelly has studied human resilience extensively through the University of Oklahoma, the University of Minnesota, Dalhousie University, and O2X Human Performance, as well as training abroad.

Kelly speaks regularly on resilience, grief, growth, and what it means to live well, especially in difficult times. His work draws from ancient truths, lived experience, and the sacred in the ordinary.

He lives in the Midwest with his wife and dogs. He loves the mountains, sun on his face, cold air in his lungs, good beer, good books, and gathering with people he loves.

ALSO BY KELLY MCCOY

Endure: A Memoir of Grief, Resilience, and Love

www.ingramcontent.com/pod-product-compliance
Lightning Source LLC
Chambersburg PA
CBHW030919140626
46545CB00016B/1558